Planning techniques
for a better future

Planning techniques for a better future

A summary of a research project
on planning for growth, redistribution
and employment

Graham Pyatt and Erik Thorbecke

Foreword by Louis Emmerij

Published with the financial support of the
United Nations Fund for Population Activities

International Labour Office   Geneva

ISBN 92-2-101552-1 (paperback)
ISBN 92-2-101553-X (hardback)

First published 1976

Printed by Presses Centrales Lausanne SA, Switzerland

FOREWORD

The theme of this volume—which is the summary of a major research project—is currently of the utmost importance. Why? Because, at a time when the developing countries are faced with mounting problems of unemployment and poverty, it marks the beginning of *systematic* thinking on development policies that bring together both growth and redistributive elements in a single framework.

We now know that developing countries will not be able to meet the basic needs of the masses of their populations within one generation if the present status quo development policies are continued—status quo in terms of the distribution of income and wealth. Past and current development planning and policies have concentrated excessively on the modern sector at the expense of increased productivity and incomes in the traditional rural and informal urban sectors where the majority of the population eke out a living. Contrary to the expectations of conventional development wisdom, the benefits of the exceptional growth rate that has occurred—an average of 5 per cent, sustained over many years—have not filtered down to the majority of the people, but have remained concentrated in the hands of a few in the modern sector of the economy. This "development route" will lead to disaster.

Of course, if we were living in a universe where time does not count, current development strategies might well be able to satisfy the basic needs of the people—if they had plenty of time to live, say 100 or 120 years! In fact, two choices are open to us: either to maintain the status quo and sacrifice three or four generations in the hitherto neglected rural and urban informal sectors; or to accept that this is humanly unacceptable and politically irresponsible and thus to change the pattern of development so that the basic needs of the poor can be met within a single generation. For this to happen high growth strategies must be pursued, coupled with more or less radical changes in the distribution of income and wealth.

All this is spelt out in some detail in the report prepared for the ILO Tripartite World Conference on Employment, Income Distribution and Social Progress and the International Division of Labour, *Employment, growth and basic needs : a one-world problem*. In that report it is argued that development planning and policies should include, as an explicit goal, the satisfaction of an absolute level of basic needs. Such a proposal goes further than concentrating ad hoc development measures on the poorest groups of the population. Meeting the basic needs of the poor within an acceptable time must become the heart and soul of economic and social development policy planning. Employment enters into a needs-oriented strategy both as a means and as an end. Employment yields an output. It provides an income. And it gives the recognition of being engaged in something worth while.

Although I am personally convinced that this basic needs orientation to development will be the conventional wisdom of tomorrow, there may still be many today who believe that the case is not argued carefully enough and that we lack a conceptual and information framework for its proper implementation.

Elaborating such a framework is exactly what Graham Pyatt and Erik Thorbecke start to do in the following pages. In that sense they are initiating the scientific underpinning of a basic needs approach to development—i.e. a growth-cum-redistribution development strategy. Because distributional questions are not part of the conceptual framework that underlies present national income statistics, a large part of this book is necessarily devoted to an adaptation of this conceptual framework so that "national accounts might now be focused on the war on poverty". The framework proposed is the social accounting matrix (SAM). I believe this to be an important contribution leading towards more systematic thinking on one of the main problems of our age.

Equally important is the careful reasoning of the two authors when they set out the policy rationale of their approach. They observe that, in facing the challenge of eradicating absolute poverty through meeting the basic needs of the population, there should be a wide-ranging search for policies which is not circumscribed by political prejudice. They also point out that a static redistribution which is radical only in appearance should be avoided. For example, consumption transfers will alleviate the plight of the poor in the short term but may make everybody worse off in the medium and longer term because such redistributions do not affect the structure of production and resources. Consumption transfers can have an adverse effect on the rate of capital accumulation and hence the rate of economic growth in *all* sectors will slow down. What we should be looking for, therefore, is a policy which will redirect investment opportunities and flows in order to put at the disposal of the poor the capital to increase their incomes.

Graham Pyatt and Erik Thorbecke are realistic enough to see the necessity of underlining that the ownership of wealth and the distribution of land and education are central to questions of growth and inequality. They correctly draw attention to the fact that "the reallocation of assets by government policy has proved to be crucial in the history of certain countries (for instance, Japan) and therefore definitely fall within the framework that interests us, which refers to an economy in which prices have an important role in the allocation process but are not paramount".

It will be obvious from the foregoing that the Pyatt-Thorbecke volume is consistent with and elaborates upon *Employment, growth and basic needs : a one-world problem.* There the Director-General of the ILO defends the thesis that the productive mobilisation of the unemployed and underemployed plus the higher productivity of the working poor are essential means of ensuring both a level of output high enough to meet basic needs targets and its proper distribution, and draws attention to the fact that the redistribution of the ownership of or access to land and other productive resources is also likely to be, in many countries, a major means of raising the level of productivity of the working poor. At the same time he points out that such strategies imply quite high levels of investment without which there would be neither growth nor meaningful redistribution.

It is important to stress that it was in 1973 that the authors began their main research project on planning for growth, redistribution and employment, of which this book is a summary. It has therefore lived a life of its own, independent of the preparations for the ILO World Employment Conference. It is accordingly all the more gratifying to see how much the main thrust of Pyatt's and Thorbecke's work, as reflected in the present volume, and of the World Employment Conference basic document coincide and support each other. I can only express the hope that this volume is but the first in a series devoted to the further elaboration of the concept of a basic needs approach to development and its implications.

LOUIS EMMERIJ

CONTENTS

CONTENTS

PREFACE

It is a very great pleasure for us to thank the International Labour Office for its support of our work. This has been carried out over the past three years under the aegis of the World Employment Programme, with which we have been associated since its early days in 1970. Our major research project on planning for growth, redistribution and employment, which we are now completing, owes a great deal to that experience. Dr. Louis Emmerij's invitation to prepare this summary of it is especially welcome since, while our main work is essentially technical in nature, its message is intended to have a much wider relevance. Our research has led us to alter our perception of contemporary development issues: it may similarly serve others as a catalyst for the evolution of their own ideas.

In expressing our thanks to our friends and colleagues in the ILO, and more especially to those working within the World Employment Programme, we must mention in particular Antoinette Béguin, Felix Paukert, Gerry Rodgers and Yves Sabolo. They have encouraged our endeavours and supported them in many ways, over a long period. Not least, they have shown much patience during the considerable time we have spent on our research. Accordingly our sincere thanks are due to them and to numerous other friends and colleagues in the ILO. We are sure, however, that they will not feel in any way slighted by our saying that we owe most to Louis Emmerij. The decision to undertake our research came from a discussion between the three of us; and to sustain it subsequently has required time, patience and resources. Whatever the shortcomings of the final result may be, we could not have had better support for our endeavours.

At this point, as academics, we would like to thank our respective universities—Warwick and Iowa State—for making our collaboration with the ILO possible. Recently we have moved—Pyatt to the World Bank and Thorbecke to Cornell University. Both institutions have inherited our

1

undertaking with us : both have given us every opportunity to complete it in our own way. Former and present colleagues have offered helpful advice and comments. In particular, through the World Employment Programme and in other ways, we have been able to exchange ideas with colleagues at the Institute of Development Studies, University of Sussex (United Kingdom) and in the World Bank in Washington, DC. Some of them have examined a similar set of issues in their book *Redistribution with growth* [1], which parallels our own thinking at several points. At the same time it is a point of departure for us, and in acknowledging our debt to its authors we hope that they will find our contribution of some interest.

Last and not least, we are grateful for the editorial assistance of Rachel Weaving. The stylistic shortcomings which remain, however, are to be blamed solely on the authors : because of its technical nature the presentation of the material contained in this summary made great demands on us, and consequently we beg the reader's indulgence if we have not always succeeded in conveying technical concepts clearly and unambiguously.

---

[1] H. Chenery, M. S. Ahluwalia, C. L. G. Bell, J. H. Duloy and R. Jolly : *Redistribution with growth* (London, Oxford University Press, 1974).

BACKGROUND AND OBJECTIVES

1

INTRODUCTION

Our major research project on planning for growth, redistribution and employment is an attempt to understand how the interaction of different forces within a developing economy determines its progress. The main emphasis is on the links between growth, inequality and employment, and not least on how the extent of poverty and changes in it are related to familiar issues of savings and investment, balance of payments, production and distribution. The approach to these questions is that of the economic planner and, at one level, the intention is to evaluate existing planning methods and to propose new ones which give an insight into the inter-dependencies within an economy. The purpose of many of the arguments is to illustrate how different aspects of development are interwoven, and hence to ascertain the methods that are needed to analyse the issues and to evaluate policy in a planning framework. These are largely technical matters and our research is accordingly technical in nature. In this survey of the main research project we attempt to present some of the major elements of the proposed framework in a more readily understandable form and to show its operational usefulness in policy formulation.

While the work is mainly technical, its context is one of practical and urgent development problems and the need to identify policies capable of resolving these problems. A comprehensive planning framework and data system are built in order that the way in which the living standards of different groups within society are determined and the roles they play in the process of economic development may be perceived. From this we try to obtain a better appreciation of those forces which create a dynamic for growth and those which leave behind, in poverty, substantial fractions of the population. To the extent that these forces can be identified, the analysis leads to policy proposals and some insights into the extent to which a country can make progress on the basis of its own resources.

We are naturally well aware of the limitations of an approach which is essentially economic to issues which have equally important historical, sociological and political dimensions. At the same time there should not be any need to defend it. The complex factors at work in a developing society derive in part from economic considerations. By analysing this part—and not forgetting that the other parts exist—our hope is to arrive at a better understanding of the whole and to reduce the scope for prejudging issues. A technical understanding of the economic aspects provides some firmer ground as a vantage point from which to view the full complexity of the problems. While we make no claim to having established this firmer ground, results so far available suggest at least that it exists, and that further efforts to secure a footing are likely to be well justified. Until recently, the professional literature in economics has given limited attention to the question of distribution and inequality. Accordingly much remains to be done, and the study is offered as a contribution to it. Many of the issues which are taken up lead to specific suggestions for further inquiry, the results of which can build on the foundations which it has been possible to lay down so far.

The comprehensive employment strategy missions organised by the International Labour Office as part of the World Employment Programme have had a substantial influence on our thinking. We have participated in three of them [1], and one of us has contributed to the evaluation of their achievements. [2] The challenge that they take on is enormous and we are not concerned here with debating their successes and shortcomings. The relevant point for us is rather that these missions have asked questions and sought policy solutions in dimensions which, while not new in themselves, are novel in the sense that there is no established quantitative framework within which they can be analysed. It is this fact that has been the basis of our work, since it is our firm belief that methods can be pushed forward to the point that planning and policy evaluation may have a sounder basis, in terms of both the realism of what is proposed and the dimensions of reality which are captured.

Our starting point has been the need to make explicit from the outset that what interests us most is the living standards of different groups within a society. An initial problem, therefore, has been to examine the possibility of measuring living standards and to set these measures in a

---

[1] Pyatt in Sri Lanka and Iran ; Thorbecke in the Philippines.

[2] Erik Thorbecke : "The employment problem : a critical evaluation of four ILO comprehensive country reports", in *International Labour Review* (Geneva, ILO), May 1973 ; reprinted in ILO : *Strategies for employment promotion* (Geneva, 1973).

comprehensive empirical framework and data system which shows numerically what is going on in any economy and how the living standards of different groups are related both to each other and to other aspects of economic activity. The United Nations System of National Accounts [1] does not do this, although the scheme can be related to the complementary System of Social and Demographic Statistics to achieve the desired end. [2] Thus, while we have serious reservations about the usefulness and operational relevance of many of the classification systems recommended by the United Nations, the Organisation has nevertheless made some important contributions to the technical problems of definitions and sources.

In order to demonstrate that an integrated picture could be obtained from information at present available in developing countries, a study of data in Sri Lanka was undertaken as a preliminary to our main work. [3] The results of this study and of subsequent work forming part of our main research could combine to establish a factual basis for planning which sets questions of individual living standards in their proper place, i.e. at the centre of the major national economic data systems. [4] These studies demonstrated that a factual basis could be built to sustain important parts of our analysis.

Consequently, one of our main recommendations is that work on national data systems can and should be reorganised so that planning can be concerned with poverty and inequality as well as with growth. An important part of our work is concerned with suggesting appropriate classification schemes and placing the relevant facts on a consistent basis to measure and analyse jointly the determinants of growth, income distribution and employment. Clearly, the prevailing informational systems used by policy makers could be greatly improved in the above respect.

Data schemes and systems do not exist independently of a conceptual framework. The reason why national income statistics do not contain an

---

[1] United Nations : *A System of National Accounts,* Studies in methods, Series F, No. 2, Rev. 3 (New York, 1968 ; Sales No. E.69.XVII.3).

[2] idem : *Towards a System of Social and Demographic Statistics,* Studies in methods, Series F, No. 18 (New York, 1975 ; Sales No. E.74.XVII.8).

[3] F. G. Pyatt and A. R. Roe : *Social accounting methods for development policy and planning : a case study of Sri Lanka* (London, Cambridge University Press, forthcoming).

[4] Earlier work in Iran opened up this possibility (see G. Pyatt, J. Bharier, R. M. Lindley, R. Mabro and Y. Sabolo : *Methodology for macro-economic projections* (Geneva, ILO, 1973 ; mimeographed—World Employment Programme paper for restricted distribution only) ; the study of Sri Lanka proved that it could be done ; and a subsequent exercise in Swaziland has confirmed that the success in Sri Lanka could be repeated. (The Swaziland study was stimulated by the interest of staff in the United Kingdom Ministry of Overseas Development in the report on Sri Lanka.)

integrated statement of living standards for different groups is that distributional questions are not part of the conceptual framework which underlies them : the framework is preoccupied with growth. Correspondingly, separate statistics on income distribution imply a conceptual framework which regards inequality as a separate issue and a more equal distribution of income as a policy objective in its own right. Our concern to bring the two sets of data together in an integrated whole reflects the fact that their inter-relationship is essential. The crux of the problems facing many developing countries concerns the potential conflicts between policies to encourage growth and those which will do something in the short term to ameliorate the lot of the poorest members of society. If these conflicts are to be understood we need a conceptual framework which embraces them simultaneously and focuses on the links between them, both actual and potential. A general data framework is then needed to serve the conceptual framework, and not as an end in itself. [1]

A conceptual framework which brings together growth and inequality in a comprehensive way is the main theme of our research. The framework itself is modular, consisting of a set of inter-related subsystems as described in Chapter 2. Since it incorporates a large set of policy measures, the alternative effects of different development strategies (i.e. different packages of policy measures) on growth, equity and employment can be analysed quantitatively, as shown in Chapter 3.

Since ours is an economic framework, it is limited by its failure to embrace political considerations as well as by its own internal shortcomings. It has already been suggested that we do not see this separation of economic and political perspectives as a major deficiency, although we recognise that others may disagree. It is useful, therefore, to set out at this point the attitude to political factors which is adopted and the sense in which we have tried to take cognisance of them.

POLICY OBJECTIVES AND POLICY FEASIBILITY SPACE

The most obvious interface between economic and political considerations is with respect to objectives. In the conventional view the role of an economist is to work out the development paths that are feasible, given available resources, and it is for the politicians to decide which of these should be chosen. For a number of reasons this has to be an oversimplifica-

---

[1] This emphasis should not be lost in the subsidiary point that the organisation of the facts in an integrated scheme can, of itself, stimulate constructive thought on the crucial issues that policy makers need to tackle.

tion. First, there are so many potential choices that they cannot all be examined. In practice, therefore, planning tends to ignore certain possibilities, often on the grounds that they are thought to be politically unacceptable. In our approach we recognise a political constraint on policy to the extent that the conceptual framework is not designed with radical changes in political and social institutions in mind. But at the same time the ownership of wealth and the distribution of land and educational and training opportunities are central to questions of growth and inequality. The reallocation of assets by government policy has proved to be crucial in the history of certain countries (for instance, Japan) and therefore definitely fall within the framework that interests us, which refers to an economy in which prices have an important role in the allocation process but are not paramount. Similarly, the extent of public ownership and government regulation is taken as a variable within the framework and not as a datum. This reflects the fact that the role of both the public and the private sectors raises crucial questions on which a better economic understanding is needed. Accordingly we do not rule out discussion of them, even though such issues may be sensitive politically.

A second consideration affecting the breadth of our approach is its central and fundamental concern for the living standards of different groups within the population. One of the main reasons for disaggregating the population is to identify poverty groups—such as landless labour and the urban unemployed—in order to find policies which could raise their living standards. At the same time we need to consider other, more affluent groups, since it is the interplay of their respective contributions to the economy and their behaviour which determines, in association with other factors, the way in which an economy evolves. We therefore subdivide the household sector into homogenous socioeconomic groups with the aim of understanding how their different living standards are determined and how they relate to each other in economic terms.

Disaggregating the household sector according to socioeconomic characteristics is essential if questions of growth and inequality are to be understood. It has strong roots in classical political economy, going back at least 300 years. Yet it seems to have been lost sight of. The technical basis of our work derives from taking this as the starting point and tracing how each subsystem of an economy, and hence the whole, needs to be looked at from this perspective. Conflicts between growth and equality translate into conflicts between the interests of different groups as a result, while policies which support both do not necessarily benefit all groups equally.

One consequence of this approach is that it leads to a framework which is more relevant to political issues and hence can contribute construc-

7

tively to political debate. In this way it is more sensitive and may even be less acceptable to vested interests. However, we have no golden rule as to how much inequality there should be. In the first instance the approach is directed at what the inequalities are, how they are inter-related, and the way in which policy instruments and structural reforms might influence them.

While we have no specific rule to suggest concerning inequality, our position on poverty is less ambivalent. At any one moment there are members of society who lack basic minimum needs. What these constitute will depend on time and place as well as on social and ethical norms. There is, therefore, no absolute poverty level [1]; but in any society there is a lower limit to what is acceptable as a decent living standard. Where the line is drawn is a measure of resource availability and civilisation, given the implication that to raise individuals above it calls for the highest priority. Thus, while the definition of a poverty line is ambiguous, the recognition that there are poor people, that the poor are deprived and hence that poverty alleviation calls for immediate action is a crucial consideration which must be included in a planning framework.

In this spirit our conceptual framework gives explicit recognition to poverty. For a given definition of what is minimal, the framework is concerned with the incidence of poverty in each socioeconomic group. Hence the implications of alternative "poverty lines" can be explored, not least relative to the prospects for doing something about it. Alternative strategies are to be judged in part, therefore, with respect to alternative definitions of poverty and what they propose should be done to reduce it. In some countries the minimum will need to be drawn at a pitifully low level if a basis for constructive action is to be found. This is because the alleviation of poverty in its extreme forms requires subsidies from rich to poor and a reallocation of scarce resources in a way which is unlikely to have any immediate justification in terms of economic efficiency. Development strategies which derive from the single-minded pursuit of economic growth can reduce poverty in the long run. But such an approach can also imply an abuse of the notion of what poverty is : poverty is a human condition which society recognises and acts to alleviate relative to its resources. The logic, therefore, is that the absence of action, domestically or internationally, implies a lack of recognition or a lack of the resources to do a great deal about it. The elimination of poverty provides a much

---

[1] There is, of course, a necessary minimum for survival. However, we assume that policy makers are concerned with a lower limit to living standards which represents a discernible improvement beyond this edge of existence.

more specific policy target than simply a reduction in the inequality of the income distribution. In this way poverty is distinct from inequality.[1]

Since ours is an economic framework, whereas poverty depends on social values, the approach we have adopted is to set out a framework in which the implications of alternative definitions can be explored. Their evaluation is not something we wish to prejudge. The approach is therefore to set up the mechanisms for monitoring how both poverty, inequality and total output are likely to be influenced by internal policies and external events. A whole set of policy navigation tables can therefore be derived relating alternative packages of policy measures to resulting combinations of policy objectives and, more particularly, equity (i.e. the living levels of the poor) and growth (the level of GNP over time).

The policy feasibility space reflecting the combination of developmental objectives which can be obtained by various packages of policy measures should be thoroughly evaluated. The choice among the alternatives is then a second step to which we return shortly. Meanwhile, however, there should be a wide-ranging search of policies which is not circumscribed by political prejudice. This is because the choice of strategy needs to be informed by what the alternatives are. The costs and benefits of particular actions have to be known before a reasonable decision on their merits can be taken. In particular, the creation and/or maintenance of incentives within the economic system must be given due weight.

A consequence of this approach is that the framework we have set out is very general. In fact, most of the planning models we know are special cases of the general specification adopted here. To evaluate their relevance requires a sense of how critical particular assumptions might be. The more general modular framework provides this. Within it the simpler methods which we and others have used in the past, and will continue to use in practical working situations, are evaluated. They emerge as having strengths and weaknesses (and some of the latter can be redressed), but they are all simplifications of the more comprehensive framework set out in our main research. In this sense, then, the latter puts them in perspective and suggests the next steps which are likely to be most rewarding if practical planning is to come to terms with poverty, employment and inequality, while retaining its concern with economic growth.

Thus in its broadest context our framework provides methods for the design and evaluation of policies which presuppose an interest in what is

---

[1] Relative inequality is normally measured in terms of the Gini coefficient. Since there can be any number of income distributions all yielding the same value of the Gini coefficient, some choices would entail greater absolute poverty than others. Hence a reduction in inequality does not necessarily reduce absolute poverty.

happening to the living standards of different socioeconomic groups without imposing any particular scheme or criterion for evaluating or choosing between alternatives. In this sense, it is presumably non-controversial. Nobody could object to the formulation of policy navigation tables.

At the same time, however, there is some merit in specifying a preference function so as to permit a choice to be made between possible alternative development paths. This preference function should reflect the relative importance of achieving major policy objectives over time. If aggregate growth is the sole objective of the policy maker, then by definition the latter is indifferent to the way GNP is distributed among individuals—a pound of rice is the same whoever eats it. In contrast, a more distributionally oriented preference function could be based on the principle that increases in living standards should be considered on a proportionate basis so that a gain of 1 per cent in living standards is valued equally for all individuals. Finally, a third possible preference function could give a higher relative weight to income received by the poor up to the poverty line than to income received by those who are already above the poverty line. [1]

It has already been mentioned that our approach does not necessarily require the specification of a preference or criterion function—in which case our framework would trace out the various possible development paths in the form of policy navigation tables. However, in the parts of our analysis which call for a particular criterion for evaluating alternatives, we adopt the second formulation above and in some instances the third one.

The major implication of the second criterion is that since one pound of rice would represent a larger percentage gain for a poorer person, other things being equal, the allocation should always be to the poorest. Thus, if the total income which an economy can generate were independent of the distribution of that income, we should favour a progressive policy of reallocation from rich to poor until everyone had an equal share. The fact that the size of the cake (i.e. the total income generated) is not independent of its distribution is the basic reality that our framework attempts to tackle. Different income distributions imply differences in the structure of production and assets prevailing in the economy.

In measuring performance by the average percentage gains for individuals our concern is simply to discourage policies which leave substantial fractions

---

[1] These three preference functions coincide, respectively, with *(a)* the maximisation of average income in the growth case; *(b)* the maximisation of the geometric mean income in the case of a more distributionally oriented objective function; and *(c)* weighting more heavily a relative increase in income below the poverty line than above it.

of the population in poverty : governments are assumed to be at least as concerned to encourage a given percentage increase in the living standards of the less affluent as they are for the more fortunate.

In a fundamental sense, our conception of economic and social development is the attainment of the highest standards of living for all, but more particularly for the poor members of society. Hence we are interested in growth and poverty eradication. As a minimum, and in line with preference function *(b)* referred to in the previous footnote, the welfare of each individual should be counted as contributing equally to the over-all welfare of society to reflect the principle of the fundamental equality of mankind. Hence the approach which observes this principle has been described as the "democratic" approach, and the evaluation of alternatives in terms of the percentage effect on individuals is referred to correspondingly as the "democratic criterion". [1]

No one knows how much difference it would make to the choice of a "best" policy if a country adopted the democratic criterion in policy design, because it has not as yet been tried. It is therefore not possible to say how radical or conservative the resulting strategy might be. Our framework permits only an *a priori* examination of the issues, and results are needed in particular country contexts before the potential implications can take on any substance. Meanwhile, some would argue that it is too conservative on the grounds that an increase of 1 per cent in living standards means more in welfare terms for a poor person than a rich one. This view has some appeal and is, for example, among the alternatives considered in a recent book written by staff from the Institute of Development Studies at the University of Sussex (United Kingdom) and the World Bank in Washington. [2] Indeed, there are instances where we adopt a choice criterion which is weighted towards poverty eradication as was pointed out above. Nevertheless, in general we are prepared to defend the adoption of the "democratic criterion" for at least two reasons.

The first reason for not selecting a criterion weighted even more heavily towards reducing inequality hinges on the fact that poverty and inequality are not the same thing. Concern for the poor is consistent with the acceptance of differentials among the affluent. In fact, these

---

[1] It should be recalled that the maximisation of the average (arithmetic mean income), or GNP, corresponds to using weights proportional to the individual's or group's existing share in national income (i.e. "one rupee, one vote"), whereas the maximisation of the geometric mean income implies that income growths of different individuals in society are given weights proportional to their number (i.e. "one man, one vote").

[2] See Chenery *et al., op. cit.*

differentials may be required as an incentive device to allow the affluent to contribute fully to the production process. It is one thing to modify the "democratic criterion" so as to give first priority to weighting relatively much more heavily any relative increase in income up to the poverty line—while limiting the actual application of the democratic criterion only to those income recipients above the poverty line—and quite another thing to select a more radical preference function with regard to the reduction in inequality *independently* of poverty. Since poverty eradication and inequality can be considered to be separate (although inter-related) objectives, there is nothing internally inconsistent in taking a "radical " view with regard to the desirability of poverty eradication and a "moderate" view with regard to reducing income inequality for income recipients above the poverty line.

Furthermore, a much more important element determining the extent of growth, inequality and poverty is the feasible policy space which is directly related to given packages of policy measures. Thus a more ambitious package of policy instruments and structural reforms including, for instance, a major land reform may result in a new feasibility frontier with respect to growth and equity permitting the achievement of higher levels of both than any combination of these objectives that may be obtainable with a more limited set of policy measures.

This point is illustrated in figure 1. The axes measure the living standards of two groups within society. The vertical axis measures the average living standard of the poorer half of the population, while the average living standard of the richer half is on the horizontal axis. Curve AB represents the feasible policy frontier, i.e. all the alternative combinations of these average living standards that can be achieved by different combinations of some limited set of policy instruments. Similarly, curve CD shows what may be possible if a more ambitious set of policies is considered. This second frontier, CD, must lie beyond AB, and the area ABCD represents all the new possibilities that become available as a result of expanding the range of policy measures considered. With respect to the limited set of possibilities represented by AB, our preference criterion would lead to the choice of point E. A more radical criterion would choose some point to the left of E, the extreme case being the choice of point A. If the range of policy options is now expanded, so that new possibilities in the area ABCD become available, the "democratic criterion" leads to the choice of point F. It is clear that both rich and poor are better off at F than they are at A. Hence the diagram illustrates the contention that more may be achieved by a moderate selection criterion, in association with a wide-ranging search of policies, than may result from a more radical preference function associated with a narrower view of policy options.

Figure 1. Interaction of objectives and policy packages (log scales)

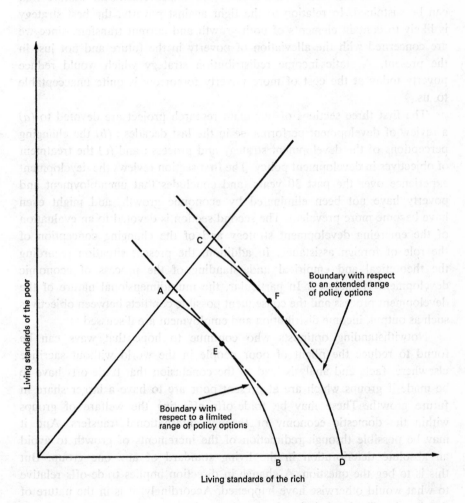

Living standards of the poor

Living standards of the rich

Boundary with respect to an extended range of policy options

Boundary with respect to a limited range of policy options

A second reason for avoiding a radical preference function with respect to objectives is that, in fact, policy makers have to be concerned not only with present achievements in terms of objectives but also with future achievements. [1] Often this is done by discounting the future, which means that less weight is given to the welfare of future generations than to contemporary well-being. We find it hard to justify discounting the future too heavily. In essence, we are looking for improvements in welfare that can be sustained. In relation to the fight against poverty, the best strategy is likely to contain elements of both growth and current transfers, since we are concerned with the alleviation of poverty in the future and not just in the present. A static income redistribution strategy which would reduce poverty today at the cost of more poverty tomorrow is quite unacceptable to us.

The first three sections of our main research project are devoted to *(a)* a review of development performance in the last decades ; *(b)* the changing perceptions of the development strategy and process ; and *(c)* the treatment of objectives in development policy. The first section reviews the development experience over the past 30 years, and concludes that unemployment and poverty have not been eliminated by economic growth, and might even have become more prevalent. The second section is devoted to an evaluation of the emerging development strategy and of the changing conception of the role of foreign assistance. In addition, the present situation regarding the theoretical and empirical understanding of the process of economic development is analysed. In particular, the multidimensional nature of the development process and the consequent possible conflicts between objectives such as output, income distribution and employment are discussed.

Notwithstanding optimists who continue to hope that ways can be found to reduce the plight of poor people in the world without sacrifice elsewhere, facts and analysis lead to the conclusion that trade-offs have to be made if groups which are at present poor are to have a larger share in future growth. These may be trade-offs affecting the welfare of groups within the domestic economy or through international transfers. And it may be possible through redirection of the increments of growth to avoid an absolute deterioration in the living standard of any one group. But this is to beg the question. A change in direction implies trade-offs relative to what would otherwise have happened. Accordingly, it is in the nature of the situation that hard choices have to be made.

---

[1] A static redistribution of income through consumption transfers, for example, would not alter the structure of production and resources in the initial period and therefore could not lead to any sustainable changes in the generation of incomes over time.

In this respect the key trade-offs from the standpoint of our study are those between output and employment, on the one hand, and output and income distribution, on the other. It is clear that, to a large extent, income distribution and employment are two sides of the same coin. A certain employment-cum-production pattern generates a unique primary income distribution and vice versa. Hence the existence of a trade-off between output and employment implies a conflict between output and income distribution as well. Whether such trade-offs do in fact prevail has been disputed. Our view is that in practice they do exist. Up to a point, economies can expand both output and employment. The precise relationship will depend on what is produced and the techniques that are chosen. Then, at some point, a conflict arises because some resources such as foreign exchange, capital or skills become so scarce that they are binding constraints. Once such a binding constraint has been reached, continued expansion of both output and employment is no longer possible and further progress in one dimension (say, employment) and a corresponding more equal income distribution has to be at the expense of some other, such as output.

This is the general situation, and it needs to be recognised. Much can be done to modify the severity of the trade-offs which constraints imply. But there is no way of avoiding them entirely unless the constraints themselves can be made to yield. Growing export markets or long-term injections of foreign capital can give a country the chance to grow without trade-offs being involved. But otherwise they are likely to emerge. While our analysis concentrates on domestic issues and policies, one aspect of the conclusions to be drawn from it is that there is a limit to what can be achieved. This limit is set by the international context. If this does not give room for growth or if a country cannot overcome the obstacles to creating a space for itself in the international trading world, then there are limits to what can be done and the need for trade-offs among things which are all desirable in themselves can dominate domestic policy discussion.

It follows from this that in some sense there are always some trade-offs to be accepted because there is always some limitation on current actions. This is why it is essential to decide what the objectives of policy should be, since the trade-offs are, by definition, restricted to those among variables which are included in the list of objectives. Specifically, we have asked the question whether employment should be an explicit objective of policy, and we have come to the conclusion that it should not.

This rejection of employment as an objective does not imply that it is unimportant : on the contrary, generating an effective demand for labour is a prime element in any attractive strategy. In that sense employment may be the crucial means towards reducing poverty and helping to achieve a more equal income distribution. Productive employment provides income to workers and thereby affects total output and income distribution. However, means and objectives should not be confused. Our objectives focus on living standards. Employment generation, *per se,* does not necessarily help widows or the old, and may suggest a régime of low wages. It does not, of itself, encourage training in new skills or suggest that wealth inequalities may need to be redressed. Yet all these things follow from a focus on living standards. For many of the world's poor the problem is not lack of work-subsistence—farmers and pedal-car drivers have plenty of it. The problem for them is rather that the work is too hard and the returns too meagre. [1]

A final qualification which should be made before we move to the more technical discussion of our framework is that we have not incorporated demographic variables endogenously in our approach. However, the mechanics of population growth can easily be incorporated in the framework so far as they are understood, and we can look to Bachue for progress in this respect. [2] However, its originator has pointed out [3] that many questions of population policy cannot be resolved without reference to the psychic satisfactions associated with family size. Only those who would deny their existence or who have not as yet obtained some appropriate means of measurement can do more than study the implications of alternative policies. In principle the subjective satisfactions of dignity in work and desired family size could be included in our measure of living standards, and hence in the objectives which policy should seek to achieve. In practice we have not done this and these omissions may be more important than our limited acknowledgement of political factors.

At this point we are ready to go into more technical matters, namely the description of our conceptual framework and data system.

---

[1] In one respect our rejection of employment as an objective in itself is not entirely satisfactory. As Sen has pointed out, one of the dimensions of employment is to have a job which gives the individual a sense of dignity which comes from feeling that he is making a worthwhile contribution (see Amartya Sen: *Employment, technology and development* (Oxford, Clarendon Press, 1975)). This is a powerful, human factor which has ramifications we have failed to consider fully. Equally, its subjective nature makes it difficult, if not impossible, to accommodate.

[2] Bachue is the generic title of research on economic, demographic and educational interactions being undertaken as part of the ILO World Employment Programme. See M. J. D. Hopkins, G. B. Rodgers and R. Wéry: *A structural overview of Bachue-Philippines* (Geneva, ILO, 1976; mimeographed—World Employment Programme paper for restricted distribution only).

[3] R. Blandy: "The welfare analysis of fertility reduction", in *The Economic Journal* (London, Macmillan), Mar. 1974.

CONCEPTUAL FRAMEWORK, DATA SYSTEM AND ANALYSIS

2

Our comprehensive planning framework is built upon two pillars : *(a)* a modular analytical framework specifying, for a set of interconnected subsystems, the major relationships between variables within and between these subsystems ; and *(b)* an elaborate complementary data and classification system. It will be seen subsequently that these two pillars can be combined together into a social accounting matrix (SAM) containing not only the comprehensive data system for any given period but the whole algebraic specification of the dynamic model linking the various variables and subsystems and permitting the derivation of future equilibrium values and, consequently, future SAMs.

As a data framework, the social accounting matrix is a snapshot at one particular moment. It provides a classification scheme for data which is useful in the light of the policy needs available to the planners. The SAM framework also incorporates explicitly various crucial transformations between variables, such as the mapping of factorial income distribution from the structure of production and the mapping of the household income distribution from the factorial income distribution.

The use of the SAM as a modular analytical framework, on the other hand, provides the natural complement to its use as a data framework by analysing and specifying the forms of the relationships underlying these transformations in the appropriate subsystems. Since many of these relationships take place over time, each subsystem (and, in a more general sense, the complete consistency framework embracing all the subsystems) explains and determines the time paths of the variables. In turn, the new equilibrium values of the variables generated by the system yield for any point in time a new data set. Furthermore, as is discussed in Chapter 3, the analytical consistency framework incorporates the policy means which can be used as levers to move the system in the desired direction—consistent with whatever (multiple) objective preference function is selected.

In what follows we shall describe, first, the modular conceptual framework which brings out explicitly, in a consistent way, the interdependence between the various parts and variables of the complete system ; second, the social accounting matrix as a data and classification system ; and third, the integration of the conceptual framework and the data system into a comprehensive SAM.

THE CONCEPTUAL PLANNING FRAMEWORK

Perhaps the simplest starting point in describing our framework as an analytical system is to recall the inter-relationship between *(a)* the structure of production ; *(b)* the distribution of the value added, generated by the production activities ; and *(c)* consumption, savings and investment. Figure 2 reflects this inter-relationship in terms of the above three links. Such a system should be internally consistent, in not only a static but also a dynamic sense. The requirements for consistency can perhaps first be described within a static setting. In this context, the static requirements are that, starting at any point in the triangle, the feedback mechanism throughout the system should yield the same initial set of values. For instance, if the starting point is a given pattern of income distribution and employment, corresponding expenditure and investment effects are implied by link 1 in the diagram. In turn, this implies a given output mix through link 2, which then translates via link 3 into a derived demand for factors and corresponding household income distribution equivalent to the one which was initially selected. This last distribution must be the same as the distribution assumed initially. Approaching these issues in a general equilibrium framework assures such consistency whereas a partial approach, focusing on some of the links only, does not. [1]

The logic underlying our modular planning framework and corresponding

---

[1] It can be noted that there is now a plethora of country studies of the partial type which explore the effects of hypothetical changes in the income distribution on the pattern of production and corresponding employment pattern. The starting point of these studies is to postulate a new—arbitrarily determined—income distribution, and then to trace through the mechanisms which move the system. Often this is confined to the effects of the new demand pattern, triggered by the exogenously selected income distribution on production without reference to the further link from production to income distribution.

Thus it means that, in terms of figure 2, these studies follow links 1 and 2. By ignoring the third link from production activities to income distribution the interdependent system is "short-circuited" at the cost of ensuring internal consistency. Incidentally, it might be noted that very few empirical studies have attempted to model that last link. One of the contributions of the present approach is, in fact, the detailed treatment of this link in the circular system shown in figure 2, as discussed subsequently.

Figure 2. The inter-relationship between production, distribution, and consumption and investment

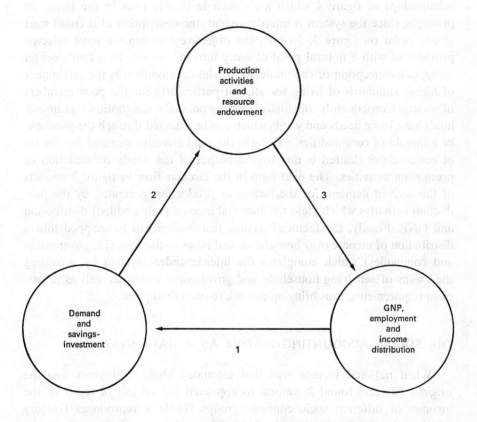

19

data system is more complex than the triangular scheme presented in figure 2. The major module of that framework, as well as the causal interdependence between the former, is given in figure 3. This last figure is, in fact, a simplified subset of the complete system which is given in figure 4 and discussed in detail in the section "Towards an integration of the conceptual planning framework and the data system" below, in which the conceptual framework and the data system are integrated into a comprehensive social accounting matrix. More specifically, figure 3 emphasises those parts and relationships of figure 4 which are drawn in double lines in the latter. In principle, since the system is interdependent, the description of it could start at any point on figure 3. In fact, the objective function we have selected provides us with a natural point of entry into the system. In a fundamental sense, our conception of economic and social development is the attainment of higher standards of living for all, but particularly for the poor members of society. Consequently, the logical starting point is a recognition that households have basic needs and wants which can be satisfied through the purchase of a bundle of commodities. [1] In turn, the total effective demand for the set of commodities desired is met by the output of the whole constellation of production activities. The next loop in the circular flow in figure 3 consists of the derived demand for the factors of production generated by the production activities which yield the factorial income (value added) distribution and GNP. Finally, the factorial income distribution can be mapped into a distribution of income over households and other institutions (i.e. government and companies) which completes the interdependent system by providing the means of satisfying household and government wants, as well as investment requirements, thus bringing us back to our initial point.

THE SOCIAL ACCOUNTING MATRIX AS A DATA SYSTEM

When national income was first estimated about 300 years ago the original pioneers found it natural to approach the subject in terms of the incomes of different socioeconomic groups. Table 1 reproduces Gregory King's estimates for England in 1688. The main part of the table shows details for different groups, covering family size, incomes, expenditure and savings. The consolidation at the foot of the table separates households with positive savings from those whose savings are negative, i.e. "decreasing the

---

[1]As figure 3 shows graphically, in addition to household expenditures on wants, investment expenditures, government consumption, net foreign demand and intermediate demand for raw materials have to be added to yield total commodity expenditures.

Figure 3. Causal interdependence between subsystems

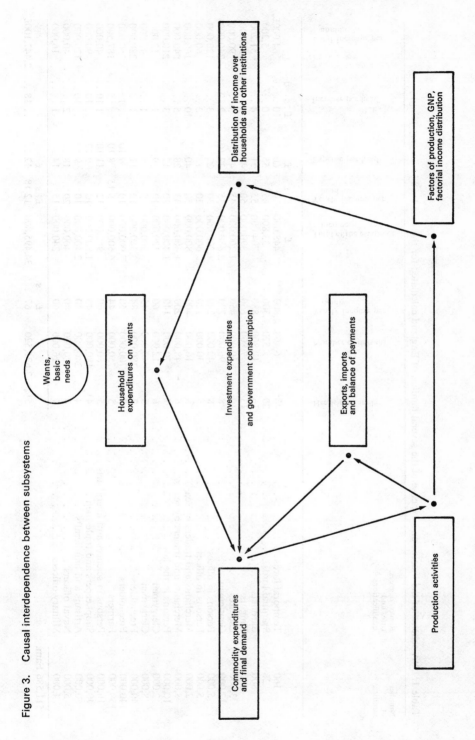

Table 1. "A scheme of the income and expense of the several families of England calculated for the year 1688" (Gregory King)

Number of families	Ranks, degrees, titles and qualifications	Heads per family	Number of persons	Yearly income per family	Total of the estates or income	Yearly income per head		Expense per head		Increase per head			Total increase per annum
				£	£	£	s	£	s	£	s	d	
160	Temporal lords	40	6,400	2,800	448,000	70		60			10		64,000
26	Spiritual lords	20	520	1,300	33,800	65		55			10		5,200
800	Baronets	16	12,800	880	704,000	55		51			4		51,200
600	Knights	13	7,800	650	390,000	50		46			4		31,200
3,000	Esquires	10	30,000	450	1,200,000	45		42			3		90,000
12,000	Gentlemen	8	96,000	280	2,880,000	35		32	10	2	10		240,000
5,000	Persons in offices	8	40,000	240	1,200,000	30		27			3		120,000
5,000	Persons in offices	6	30,000	120	600,000	20		18			2		60,000
2,000	Merchants and traders by sea	8	16,000	400	800,000	50		40			10		160,000
8,000	Merchants and traders by sea	6	48,000	200	1,600,000	33		28			5		240,000
10,000	Persons in the law	7	70,000	140	1,400,000	20		17			3		210,000
2,000	Clergymen	6	12,000	60	120,000	10		9			1		12,000
8,000	Clergymen	5	40,000	45	360,000	9		8			1		40,000
40,000	Freeholders	7	280,000	84	3,360,000	12		11			1		280,000
140,000	Freeholders	5	700,000	50	7,000,000	10		9	10			10	350,000
150,000	Farmers	5	750,000	44	6,600,000	8	15	8	10			5	187,500
16,000	Persons in sciences and liberal arts	5	80,000	60	960,000	12		11	10	1	10		40,000
40,000	Shopkeepers and tradesmen	4½	180,000	45	1,800,000	10		9	10			10	90,000
60,000	Artisans and handicrafts	4	240,000	40	2,400,000	10		9	10			10	120,000
5,000	Naval officers	4	20,000	80	240,000	20		18			2		40,000
4,000	Military officers	4	16,000	60	240,000	15		14			1		16,000
511,586 Fam.		5¼	2,675,520	67 (£ s)	34,495,800	12	18	12			18		2,447,100

Number of Families	Ranks, Degrees, Titles and Qualifications	Heads per Family	Number of Persons	Yearly Income per Family £ s	Yearly Income in general £	Income per Head £ s d	Expense per Head £ s d	Incr. or Decr. per Head £ s d	Decrease £
50,000	Common seamen	3	150,000	20 ..	1,000,000	7	7 10 ..	.. 10 ..	75,000£
364,000	Labouring people and outservants	3½	1,275,000	15 ..	5,460,000	4 10 ..	4 12 ..	.. 2 ..	127,500
400,000	Cottagers and paupers	3¼	1,300,000	6 10	2,000,000	2	2 5 ..	.. 5 ..	325,000
35,000	Common soldiers	2	70,000	14 ..	490,000	7	7 10 ..	.. 10 ..	35,000
849,000 Fam.		3¼	2,795,000	10 10	8,950,000	3 5 ..	3 9 ..		562,000£
....	Vagrants		30,000	2 ..	60,000	2	3	.. 1 ..	60,000
849,000		3¼	2,825,000	10 10	9,010,000	3 3 ..	3 7 6	.. 4 6	622,000£

So the General Account is:

Number of Families		Heads per Family	Number of Persons	£ s	£	£ s d	£ s d	£ s d	£
511,586 Fam.	Increasing the wealth of the Kingdom	5¼	2,675,520	67 10	34,495,800	12 18 ..			2,447,100£
849,000 Fam.	Decreasing the wealth of the Kingdom	3¼	2,825,000	10 10	9,010,000	3 3 ..	3 7 6	.. 4 6	622,000
1,360,586 Fam.	Net totals	4 1/20	5,500,520	32 ..	43,505,800	7 11 3	7 18 ..	.. 6 9	1,825,100£

Note: Spellings have been modernised.

wealth of the Kingdom". The majority of the population are in this latter group, but they receive less than a quarter of the total income. Among the affluent the savings rate is highest among "merchants and traders by sea" (the table lists them below "gentlemen" and "persons in offices", despite their higher income). All this is as one might expect from a knowledge of England 300 years ago. And it is pertinent to ask : how much more would we know and understand if the history of England and other countries had been recorded down the years in the format of table 1 ? The data are admittedly crude and, for all his boldness with numbers, King does not attempt to estimate the number of "vagrants" ; but he has at least approached the subject of national accounting in its most natural form, i.e. "Who gets what ?"

Economies have become more complex over the centuries from an institutional point of view. Government exists independently of "temporal and spiritual lords", etc., and many of the large commercial activities are now carried out by a corporate sector. Accordingly, a contemporary version of table 1 would have to include them. But subject to these caveats the table is as relevant today, as a basic information scheme, as it was originally. One of our chief concerns is to start with such an approach to national accounting and to follow through its implications. A particular point which arises as a result is that income inequality in less developed countries is often exaggerated relative to the situation in richer countries. This is because corporate forms of organisation are more prevalent in the latter. Their retained earnings do not appear in the personal income distribution, which accordingly seems to be more equal than it would otherwise be. Such institutional differences also influence comparisons with socialist countries. For these and other reasons, international comparisons are more meaningful when they are based on the distribution of consumption, i.e. on living standards, and not on income.

National data systems and planning models have come a long way since 1688. While the focus on distribution has been lost, there have been great strides in other respects—production, trade and accumulation are all now more or less covered in standard format, while extensions into the pattern of production interdependence and imports have added greatly to the understanding of the technical inter-relationships at work. The United Nations system has provided a scheme for covering all these and much more. But its main intellectual foundation is *A programme for growth* [1]—a work which emanates from a developed country that already has established institutions

---

[1] *A programme for growth* is the generic title of the main publications of a research team which has been working under the direction of R. Stone in Cambridge since 1960. See University of Cambridge, Department of Applied Economics : *A programme for growth*, 12 vols. (London, Chapman and Hall, 1962-   ).

and mechanisms concerned directly with distributional questions. Emphasis on growth was therefore appropriate. It is also highly relevant in poorer countries, but for them there is more at stake. Between King and Stone the main contribution to national accounting in the United Kingdom came from Keynes and was directed toward reformulating national income accounts in a way more useful to the financing of the war effort. [1] It is suggested that national accounts might now be focused on the war on poverty, while recognising that growth will be important in the strategy for winning it.

It is a well known rule that every economic model must have either an implicit or an explicit accounting framework. This rule derives from the fact that every receipt is also an expenditure, and that every income must be matched by corresponding outlays. If the model violates these rules, then the model must be wrong. The rules are the equivalent for an economist of the physicist's Law of the Conservation of Energy. They do not provide a complete specification of how an economy works but merely capture the accounting constraints that must be satisfied. As a classification scheme and arranging device for variables, the social accounting matrix constitutes a necessary and complementary step in the specification of an operationally useful planning framework.

Since we are concerned with growth, redistribution and employment, the format of the SAM framework and the corresponding accounting rules should be designed accordingly. Table 2 provides the major elements of the basic social accounting matrix. A concrete application of this framework applied to the case of Sri Lanka is given in the appendix in tables 6 and 7. Since these tables are described in detail in the appendix and are based on the actual numerical values obtaining in Sri Lanka, we can limit ourselves here to a general description of the major elements of the SAM.

Conceptually, it is through the production process that value added accruing to the various factors of production is generated. In turn, value added received by the factors complemented by and corrected for transfer payments, taxes and subsidies has to be mapped into a corresponding household income distribution. Thus, three levels or steps can be distinguished in this mapping process: *(a)* the structure of production, typically broken down into a number of production sectors or activities; *(b)* the factorial distribution of value added; and *(c)* the household distribution of income. [2] In this process of mapping the household income distribution from the streams of value added generated by the production activities, a crucial

---

[1] His 1940 Government White Paper was entitled *An analysis of the sources of war finance and an estimate of the national income and expenditure in 1938 and 1940.*

[2] These are the same links as those shown in figure 3 and discussed in the previous section.

question is that of an appropriate classification scheme for the various accounts in the SAM. If the transformation from the structure of production to the factorial, and ultimately the household, income distribution is to be performed in an operationally useful way for planning purposes, great care must be exercised in designing appropriate classification schemes for each account. This question is discussed in detail in the next section.

Thus our data system incorporates—what, incidentally, national income accounts ignore—the mechanisms that translate the generation of value added by production into the income of different types of households and other institutions. The link is provided by factors of production. The level and structure of output by the different activities generate the aggregate demand for labour of different types, natural resources and capital services. Hence, employment enters into the analysis. The stream of value added, from the production side, rewards the factors of production, with wages going to different types of labour, rent going to land and other resources, and profits to capital. In this way a picture is obtained of the factorial distribution of income which is captured in table 2 by the interface between the column entitled "production activities" and the row "factors of production" (the interface between column 6 and row 1).

Translation from the factorial distribution to the distribution of incomes across institutions, and particularly across different household groups, depends on which institutions own which factors. Thus, for example, wage payments to semi-skilled labour go to the households which provide semi-skilled labour ; rent accrues to the owners of natural resources ; and profits accrue to owners of capital. In this fashion, the distribution of wealth and assets (including skills) in terms of who owns or possesses which factors underlies the mapping of the factorial income distribution on to the household distribution. This second transformation is shown in table 2 in the interface between column 1 (factors of production) and row 2 (households), which allocates labour income to households. Furthermore, when current government transfers to domestic households (the interface between column 4 and row 2) and profits distributed to domestic households (the interface between column 3 and row 2) are added to the labour incomes of the households, the complete household income distribution is obtained. It follows that the latter can be changed either *(a)* by altering the factorial distribution ; *(b)* by changing the distribution of wealth in terms of factor ownership ; or *(c)* through a different pattern of transfer payments.

There are two further considerations which our accounting framework must embrace. First, the existence of wealth implies accumulation and hence savings to finance it. Savings also provide a difference between income and consumption for different groups in the population. It is important, therefore,

Table 2. A basic social accounting matrix (SAM)

Receipts	Expenditures							Totals
		Institutions						
		Current accounts						
	1 Factors of production	2 Households	3 Companies	4 Government	5 Combined capital account	6 Production activities	7 Rest of the world combined account	
Current accounts — 1 Factors of production						Value added payments to factors	Net factor income received from abroad	Incomes of the domestic factors of production
Institutions — 2 Households	Allocation of labour income to households	Current transfers between households	Profits distributed to domestic households	Current transfers to domestic households				Incomes of the domestic institutions after transfers
3 Companies	Allocation of operating surplus to companies			Current transfers to domestic companies			Net non-factor incomes received from abroad	
4 Government		Direct taxes on income and indirect taxes on current expenditure	Direct taxes on companies plus operating surplus of state enterprise		Indirect taxes on capital goods	Indirect taxes on inputs	Net non-factor incomes received plus indirect taxes on exports	
5 Combined capital account		Household savings	Undistributed profits after tax	Government current account surplus			Net capital received from abroad	Aggregate savings
6 Production activities		Household consumption expenditure on domestic goods		Government current expenditure	Investment expenditure on domestic goods	Raw material purchases of domestic goods	Exports	Aggregate demand = gross outputs
7 Rest of the world combined account		Household consumption expenditure on imported goods			Imports of capital goods	Imports of raw materials		Imports
Totals	Incomes of the domestic factors of production	Total outlay of households	Total outlay of companies	Total outlay of government	Aggregate investment	Total costs	Total foreign exchange receipts	

to include capital accounts in our framework, to note the amount of savings available to finance investment—who saves, and who invests. At the same time we want to dissect the commodity composition of consumption so that living standard comparisons can be made. Finally, our accounts must cover relations with the rest of the world in terms of merchandise trade, international factor and non-factor payments and international capital movements and foreign aid.

The above describes in general terms the considerations which our accounting framework must embrace and with respect to which any model must at least be consistent. Subsequently we shall return to some of these accounts, particularly the capital account, and discuss them in more detail. It will also be seen that extra dimensions and some additional accounts are needed to capture important considerations which are not made explicit in table 2.

In the meantime, table 3 shows in a more consolidated form than the previous table the mapping from the structure of production to the distribution of income. (Again, table 7 in the appendix represents an application of the format of table 3 to the case of Sri Lanka.) Table 3 is built around a central aggregate, the total income of the domestic factors of production. In the northeast quadrant we have the details of how this depends on the structure of production and factor markets. In the northwest quadrant this total income is allocated to the institutions, and particularly the households, which provide the factor services. Hence, the distribution of wealth—defined to include human skills as well as capital—underlies this northwest quadrant. In the southwest quadrant the effects of transfer payments, i.e. of profit distribution, taxation and government social security payments, are shown. As a result of these last transactions, the central aggregate is decomposed into the disposable income of the institutions including the households.

Tables 3 and 7 are useful in revealing the determinants of the income distribution. A first determinant is the structure of production and factor markets, including labour markets. Next there is the distribution of wealth, defined to include human skills, and finally the fiscal system of taxation and benefits. All three are basic elements and, as is discussed in Chapter 3, policy to influence the distribution of income needs to focus on all three of these areas. It should also be recalled that the classifications used in the table are crucial. Indeed, in the next section we discuss in detail the criteria which appear appropriate in classifying the variables included in the various accounts.

At this stage the correspondence between the data system—as represented, for instance, by the SAM in table 3—and the conceptual framework described in the previous section should become fairly obvious. Hence

Table 3. Tableau for the analysis of income distribution

		Institutions current accounts				Production activities	Rest of the world
		Households	Companies	Government	Total		
Factors of production	Labour	Allocation of labour income to households				Wages	
	Other	Allocation of surplus of unincorporated enterprises	Allocation of operating surpluses to companies			Operating surpluses	
Institutions current accounts	Totals	Distribution of factorial income over institutions before transfers			Factorial distribution of income	Value added	
	Households		Profits distributed to domestic households	Actual and imputed current transfers to households	Distribution of disposable income		Net factor incomes received from abroad
	Companies			Current transfers to domestic companies	*		Net factor incomes received from abroad
	Government	Direct taxes on income	Direct taxes on companies plus operating surpluses of state enterprises				
Rest of the world		Net non-factor incomes paid abroad			Net non-factor incomes paid abroad	Net factor incomes received from abroad	

Distribution of factorial incomes over institutions *minus* total transfer payments

= Aggregate income of the domestic factors of production.

* Aggregate income of the domestic factors of production.

tables 3 and 7 indicate explicitly the link going from the structure of production and resource endowment to the distribution of income by household type, which we reviewed previously and made explicit in figure 2 (see link 3 in figure 2). The explicit specification of this link is a primary focus of our work—particularly since it appears to have been underrated in planning models.

It is important to note, however, that in reality the structure of production and income distribution are inter-related through the interdependent system represented in figure 2. It is this causal interdependence which accounts for the substantial element of simultaneity that exists in the determination of output and incomes. It is therefore not easy to change income distribution, since its determinants are to a considerable extent woven into the structure of an economy and cannot easily be disentangled. This is a recurring theme in the analysis and an important point of emphasis for perception of the issues. It has already been pointed out that the link from income distribution to the structure of production, via the pattern of demand, has been analysed explicitly in a number of studies. [1] A change in the income distribution generates a new demand pattern which does, in turn, give rise to a new structure of production. In a nutshell, a reduction in inequality engenders a rise in the demand for necessities such as food, while reducing the consumption demand for luxury goods. Also, to the extent that necessities are produced under more labour-intensive techniques than luxury goods, the new demand pattern and resulting consumption mix tends to increase over-all employment. This inter-relationship has been described in the previous section and can be clearly seen by looking at figures 2 and 3. [2]

It has already been suggested that each of us tried previously to recognise these two-way cause-and-effect relationships in practical planning approaches. [3] The results of these early studies are reviewed in our main research as illustrations of methods which can be adopted usefully. At the same time, some of the more serious limitations of these studies have been

---

[1] See, for example, the Fourth Indian Plan ; and F. Paukert, J. Skolka and J. Maton: *Redistribution of income, patterns of consumption and employment: a case study of the Philippines* (Geneva, ILO, 1974 ; mimeographed—World Employment Programme paper for restricted distribution only).

[2] In the appendix a concrete example of the change in the final demand for coconuts in Sri Lanka on the output mix is described in some detail.

[3] See E. Thorbecke and J. K. Sengupta : *A consistency framework for employment, output and income distribution projections applied to Colombia* (Washington, DC, World Bank Development Research Centre, 1972 ; mimeographed), and Pyatt *et al.*, op. cit. The former is a model of Colombia, which attempts to evaluate the recommendations contained in the report of the ILO comprehensive employment strategy mission (ILO : *Towards full employment : a programme for Colombia* (Geneva, 1970)). The latter is a working paper produced in the context of the comprehensive employment strategy mission to Iran.

overcome in the present volume. The essence of our contribution is a recognition that living standards are an integral part of an interdependent system as described in figures 2 and 3, and an interdependent consistency framework as depicted in tables 2 and 3.

At this stage it is important to integrate more formally the conceptual framework and the data system we have just discussed into a comprehensive social accounting matrix.

TOWARDS AN INTEGRATION OF THE CONCEPTUAL PLANNING FRAMEWORK AND THE DATA SYSTEM

Figure 4 sets out the comprehensive conceptual economic framework and serves as an organising scheme for subsequent analysis. It is, as was pointed out previously, an extension of figure 3. The arrows linking different parts of the system reflect causal connections. [1] These relationships are discussed individually, or grouped into subsystems in our main research, and are to be considered as modules in a more complete system. We have more to say about some of these modules than others—either because their relevance to issues of growth, poverty and employment differs, or because of our relative ignorance of the mechanisms at work. This is especially true of a number of relationships and issues which are only meaningful within a dynamic context, such as investment theory and technical progress. Because of their importance to issues of growth and poverty, we must consider various hypotheses.

This modular approach has various advantages. It implies that the complex of interactions in figure 4 can be discussed seriatim, module by module. Our understanding of the links within certain modules may be weaker than others—reflecting inadequacies in the present situation and in the available information. In any case, the relative strength and weaknesses of the various subsystems and in the links between them are explicitly brought out in the analysis and illustrated empirically with the help of specific country case studies.

Since the initial conditions prevailing in developing countries differ significantly in terms of elements such as the socioeconomic structure, the state of development and the coverage and quality of information, a flexible approach to planning is absolutely essential. Alternative specifications of certain relationships and subsystems, depending on these initial conditions,

---

[1] The causal relationships represented by double-lined arrows are those included in the somewhat more limited system shown in figure 3.

are required. This calls for a flexible framework in which the various modules are interchangeable to fit the underlying conditions. Subsequently, in this section, the complete system depicted in figure 4 is analysed and built up module by module. At the same time, having a complete schema (as in figure 4) forces the various modules to be internally consistent.

At this stage the essential question is how to formulate this conceptual framework in such a way that it can be incorporated into a corresponding data system and social accounting matrix framework. A simple example of the latter has been given in tables 2 and 3. However, these tables did not take account of all the issues which arise and all the variables which appear in figure 4, and therefore need to be extended. The discipline of trying to convert the conceptual framework into an SAM goes a long way towards ensuring that we are dealing with measurable phenomena, and measurable relationships connecting the various variables and modules of our complete system. Accordingly, the specific questions which we have to answer before we can complete this system are : *(a)* what mechanisms are at work in figure 4 ; and *(b)* what information is needed, and what classification schemes are appropriate, in a social accounting sense, to record these mechanisms. By implication, the approach is based on an interactive treatment of *a priori* theorising and empirical measurement.

In what follows, the major modules are described and the major relationships between variables within and between subsystems are analysed. Particular attention is paid to the design of appropriate classification schemes and the best way to convert given modules into accounts, or sets of accounts, in an SAM framework. In the next section the formal translation of the modular conceptual approach into an SAM framework is undertaken.

The major modules presented below are : *(a)* households and living standards ; *(b)* savings, investment and the flow of funds subsystems ; *(c)* final demand and its link with production ; and *(d)* the structure of production and asset ownership and its relationship to income distribution and employment. It should be noted that, since figure 4 depicts an interactive system of mostly simultaneous relationships, the starting point for this discussion is largely arbitrary. Given our concern for the living standards of different socioeconomic groups, we chose to begin with this module.

Households and their living standards

The first point to make is that conventional treatments which subdivide households by income level are not very helpful for a number of reasons. The most important of these is that policy has to be directed to particular groups which are identifiable directly in policy terms. Examples are semi-

Figure 4. The modular conceptual framework

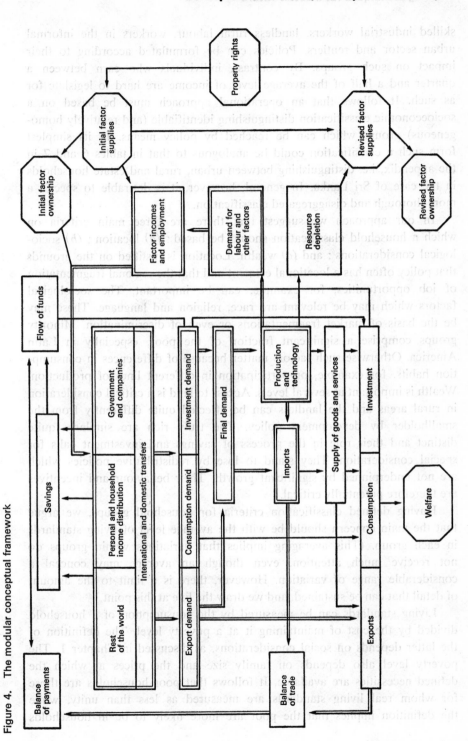

skilled industrial workers, landless rural labour, workers in the informal urban sector and rentiers. Policies can be formulated according to their impact on such groups. By contrast, individuals who earn between a quarter and a half of the average level of income are hard to legislate for as such. It follows that an operational approach must be based on a socioeconomic classification distinguishing identifiable (and relatively homogeneous) groups which can be reached by policy means. In its simplest form such a classification could be analogous to that in tables 6 and 7 in the appendix, i.e. distinguishing between urban, rural and estate households in the case of Sri Lanka. In general, however, it is desirable to specify a more thorough and disaggregated classification.

In our approach we suggest that there are three main criteria on which a household classification should be based : *(a)* location ; *(b)* sociological considerations ; and *(c)* wealth. Location is justified on the grounds that policy often has a locational element and that the regional fragmentation of job opportunities, for example, can be important. The sociological factors which may be relevant are race, religion and language. These may be the basis of market fragmentations or even of discrimination. Minority groups comprise a significant fraction of the poor, especially in Latin America. Otherwise such factors matter because of differences in consumption habits, for example, or participation in different lines of production. Wealth is important at several levels. Access to land is a critical consideration in rural areas and the landless can be affected quite differently from the smallholder by development policy. The truly rich are similarly quite distinct and their role in the process of savings and investment calls for special consideration. They stand to lose by redistributive policies which are not underpinned by significant growth. Their behaviour and incentives are therefore potentially critical.

Having defined classification criteria for household groups, we argue that the main concern should be with the average level of living standards in each group. (This averaging implies that variations within groups do not receive much attention, even though an average may conceal a considerable range of variation. However, there is a limit to the amount of detail that can be sustained, and we draw the line at this point.)

Living standards can be measured by the consumption of a household divided by the cost of maintaining it at a poverty level. The definition of the latter depends on social considerations, as discussed in Chapter 1. The poverty level also depends on family size and the prices at which the defined necessities are available. It follows that poor households are those for whom real living standards are measured as less than unity, while the definition implies that the poor are more likely to be in households

34

where dependency ratios are high, i.e. in which each earner has to support an above-average number of old people or children.

At this point it is worth noting that transfer payments between institutions are a determinant of their disposable incomes and, hence, their living standards. If government raises revenue by taxing necessities, this will tend to make poverty more prevalent. Conversely, well chosen subsidies can ease the problem greatly. The provision of free services of health and education should be allowed for in the calculation of living standards. If these are concentrated on middle-class urban groups (which are approximately equivalent to skilled industrial workers), they will not be reducing inequality. But if free schooling is provided disproportionately in favour of the poor, some of the imbalance is being redressed. This may or may not be a good thing, depending on the indirect consequences, which have to be analysed within the complete system in a dynamic context.

Numerous technical difficulties exist in relating household groups and their living standards to the over-all welfare of a society. Solutions are proposed which give a specific expression to the link at the foot of figure 4 from consumption to present welfare. They lead to the use of the geometric mean of living standards, i.e. to the "democratic" criterion discussed in Chapter 1.[1] There are also technical difficulties in the link from household incomes to the consumption component of final demand in figure 4. This, we have seen, depends on the extent of inequality. In our formulation it is made to depend explicitly on poverty within household types and on inequality in average living standards between them.

This "household" module gives specific answers to various questions : how to disaggregate households ; what is meant by poverty ; how inequality and welfare are to be treated ; and how consumption demand is generated. The particular mechanisms proposed give substance to the general point that the way households spend their money implies something about their preferences and welfare, and hence about the appropriate means of measuring the extent to which benefits accrue to different household types as a result of development. The result is an index—the geometric mean of living standards—which makes more sense than national income as a measure of social progress.

---

[1] Maximising the geometric mean of incomes is equivalent to using the democratic criterion of choice among alternative strategies. Under certain circumstances, this criterion can be modified and "poverty weights" used instead. The key question is, of course, that poverty alleviation ought to be sustainable in the medium and long term.

Savings, investment and the flow of funds

Having set out a taxonomy of the household sector and analysed consumption expenditure, we now turn to savings and investment. It is entirely inadequate to treat this subject in terms of an over-all balance between the two. In the absence of credit institutions, the investments of each household type, of companies and of government must be financed by their own savings. Moreover, the credit institutions which exist may well channel funds *away* from rural areas towards urban industrial projects. Accordingly, there is a tendency for wealth to accumulate in the modern sector more rapidly than elsewhere. The resulting imbalance is a cause of inequality. It does not necessarily follow that the flow should be reversed, since little progress is made by socially less productive investments. The point is that if no credit institutions are available to deal with the small farmer, socially desirable investment opportunities are missed to the extent that the farmer cannot finance them himself. This problem is compounded by the fact that the relatively poor individual lacks collateral to secure a loan. Hence, without wealth, it is difficult to accumulate, even though the opportunities for profitable investment may exist.

The limitations on the flow of funds are reflected in the fact that most savings and investment are the results of simultaneous decisions within households or unincorporated business. For this reason it is not enough that savings should match investment in total—to a large extent the investor should be able to supply the necessary funds himself. [1]

These considerations regarding the relationship between savings and investment are important for our analysis. We are doubtful about the evidence which suggests that greater equality reduces personal savings. But such changes in income distribution will alter the pattern of who saves and hence who invests at the household level. Moreover, any change in profit levels will most probably alter the investment of private companies. In these respects, therefore, inequality and economic growth are intimately connected. Profits must be available to finance investment if private domestic companies are to play a leading role in growth.

But there are alternatives, among them private overseas investment (which brings in expertise also) and foreign aid to finance public investment. Both operate through international capital transactions and in part explain the link between balance of payments and flow of funds at the top of figure 4.

---

[1] In most developing countries scarce foreign exchange is a binding constraint on investment. But there are further constraints on investment *within* a particular country, because of internal limitations on access to credit.

Yet another alternative is to finance public investment, including investment in state corporations, from domestic funds. But here there is a difficulty. Public enterprise rarely runs at an over-all profit, often for good reasons. Prices are held down to provide basic services at subsidised levels, thus reducing poverty. Externalities might be generated so that efficiency prices are below costs. Furthermore, the lack of profits may also be due to the familiar administrative inefficiencies. But whatever the cause, the fact that government can rarely finance its own investment from current surpluses implies that it must borrow, with the potential danger of inflationary consequences. This borrowing, in turn, implies less real investment elsewhere in the economy, and the over-all achievement may be better or worse as a result. The main concern is that different patterns of flow of funds imply different sorts of investment, and that the institutional arrangements in capital markets can preclude some patterns of credit creation which would otherwise help to build up the asset base of poorer members of society. Thus investment demand in figure 4 depends on the flow of funds as well as being a determinant of it.

The central role played by assets and their distribution emerges at this point. The link between them and the distribution of factor incomes appears in the northwest corner of table 3 (specifically as the allocation of labour income to different skills and of the surplus of incorporated and unincorporated enterprises), and again in figure 4 as the arrow from "initial factor ownership" leading into domestic incomes. Increments to these assets are represented by investment, in which we include investment in human skills through training and education, as well as factories, offices and roads. If, therefore, income distribution is to be changed through encouraging asset accumulation by the poorest at above-average rates, either the poorest must be provided with credit or they must be able to finance investment from their own savings. If the latter were possible it is unlikely they would be so poor. The former may require new institutions and a diversion of resources from other investment opportunities. Power politics may preclude this. If not, the question remains whether investments which provide assets for the poor will generate as many social benefits as could be derived from other investment opportunities which have to be forgone. It is this potential conflict which can lead to trade-offs between growth and reduced inequality. Equally, some strategies may be conducive to both. We expand on some of the operational and policy implications of this question in Chapter 3.

Final demand and its link with production

Consumption, investment and export demands make up the final demands on production activities and hence determine levels of output and imports. A number of technical issues arise at this stage. A way into them is to note that the capacities of different production activities are an important determinant of their ability to respond to increased demand. If capacity is insufficient, increased demand can spill over into imports or be choked off by price increases. There are no general rules. Most development planning models make strong assumptions regarding the above relationship and our concern has been to set out a more flexible treatment which allows the link between final demand and output to be handled with greater sensitivity. Since the treatment of this link is a highly technical area, the details are avoided here. However, some of the implications in this link are very relevant. The first point to make is that prices are determined endogenously within the general framework rather than being specified separately in advance. For some goods demand is very insensitive to price (or price-inelastic), so that the recent rises in oil prices and in the price of manufactured goods did not result in dramatic falls in quantities imported, but rather in large balance of trade deficits. For other goods demand is highly elastic, so that relatively small changes in price radically alter quantities. By allowing imports to be sensitive to prices in varying degrees, our approach makes it possible to explore how tariffs and quotas influence the economy and to ascertain the optimal exchange rate policy to adopt. This may seem a long way from questions of poverty and inequality ; but if production is restricted for lack of spare parts or raw materials, employment must drop. Lack of foreign exchange may mean food shortages when countries are not self-sufficient, and the general restriction on both production and incomes which follows from a balance of payments constraint may be the reason why output has to be sacrificed to obtain more jobs.

The extent to which an economy relies on imports depends on the structure of demand relative to production, i.e. on how much import substitution has already taken place and the scope for further developments along these lines. The latter depends in turn on the resource base of the economy and, more generally, on its comparative advantage in trade with others. To answer such questions it is essential to know how prices are determined within the economy.

Since prices are determined within our analytical framework, the design of fiscal policy can be explored. Such policy instruments as direct and indirect taxes, export subsidies and public utility pricing policy all improve or impair the performance of the economy relative to its objectives. We have not undertaken a specific country study to evaluate these issues, but it seems that at some point the poorest of the poor can be helped only by fiscal transfers. The relevant questions, then, are how transfer policies should be designed for maximum effect, and what their costs are in other respects. We have tried to provide a framework for tackling these issues as indicated in Chapter 3.

Another aspect of our treatment of the way in which demand translates into production is that it reveals where capacity is short. This is important for recognising the investment opportunities in an economy—the lines of activity which might be expanded and the new activities which might be started. Alternative plans can consequently be evaluated on the basis of shortages in current production capacities.

The structure of production and resource ownership and their relationship with income distribution and employment

The classification of production activities is crucial in deriving the pattern of income distribution and of employment. Dualism in development means that there are virtually two (or more) economies operating side by side, and largely independently of each other. Just what the linkages are and how much dualism may exist can only be perceived if we have appropriate classifications. For example, if all retail trade is treated as a single category, there is no way of knowing how far the expenditures of modern sector households "trickle down" into demand for the services of traditional unskilled labour. One can guess that the answer is, "very little". But unless production is classified with reference to the level of technology and the form of organisation, it is highly likely that the extent of dualism will be understated. Thus an inappropriate classification of production activities is likely to lead to excessive optimism about the extent to which a strategy that concentrates on growth of the modern sector will ultimately benefit all members of society. Consequently, a great deal of analytical and empirical work was done in our main research to formulate an operationally useful classification of production activities.

The analysis has now covered all but the links on the right-hand side of figure 4. The detailed discussion has built up from the distribution of income to the structure of production and included both balance of payments and flow of funds considerations. This involves some extensions of traditional methods. The outstanding issues are less often discussed in a planning context. They include employment and wealth.

Of course, many development plans refer to expected job creation. But

they do not give employment a central place, usually working back from
output projections using expected labour/output ratios. We see employment
as a much more integral part of the economy. In these terms there is a
limited basis of knowledge to work on, starting with the question of what
determines wages for different types of labour. Since we do not have a
neat answer, our approach takes relative wages as fixed in the first instance.

At given wages the demands for labour of different types are derived
from the levels of output of the various production activities. At the same
time labour supplies depend on the total population and its skills and the
past educational policies of government. The demand for, and the supply
of, different skills come together in labour markets. The result is that
some people get jobs and others do not. For the unskilled especially,
underemployment rather than open unemployment is the main consequence,
since work is often casual and sporadic. In rural areas it has a large
seasonal element. Thus there are few who are unemployed in a formal
sense : in the absence of social security payments, few can afford it.

In considering labour markets, we recognise skills as being part of
the basic wealth possessed by different types of household. In these terms
it is most useful to think of labour supply as deriving from the age, sex and
educational structure of the population. Demand, on the other hand, is
most naturally expressed in terms of jobs by occupation in different labour
markets. Thus before we can ask how demand and supply interact, we
have to reconcile these different categories. Our suggestions for so doing
put an added strain on data requirements. This underlines the fact that
information on labour markets and manpower is sparse, essentially as a
result of neglect over the years.

The details of the approach to labour markets which we adopt are not
presented here. Their outcome is a formulation which recognises four
important points. First, equilibrium in labour markets can be brought about
through *(a)* adjustment of unemployment and underemployment rates in
the typical case of excess supplies ; *(b)* adjustments in output when, for
example, key skills are scarce ; and *(c)* adjustments in wage rates. The last
of these three is an alternative to the first two. Our view is that in practice it
plays a role only in the long term. Second, the formulation recognises the
importance of both education and experience in determining job opportunities
and earnings. This corresponds to observed statistical relations which find
these variables to be important. Third, a basis for migration is derived
from the analysis which corresponds with the observed phenomenon
whereby educated young males are found to be more successful than others
in obtaining work subsequent to a move. And finally, the formulation
yields ways of evaluating the prospective benefits to people from being

better fed and better educated in terms of their expected earnings ability. Thus many of the important issues in labour market analysis are tackled, if not resolved. We return to the whole question of markets for factors of production and income and employment determination in Chapter 3, within a policy context.

Returning now to figure 4, it can be seen that the interaction of demand for factors and available supplies generates the factorial income distribution and the pattern of employment, which represent major determinants of the distribution of household and personal income. This link corresponds to the northeast quadrant of table 3, while the question of who owns the various factors underlies the northwest quadrant. Thus the modules are complete when we have specified the determinants of profits (or operating surplus) for each of the production activities—a question to which we now turn.

There is no easy answer to the question of what determines profits, and our approach allows for the interplay of various forces. Our starting point is prices, since the question can be translated into the mark-up of costs which is used to determine selling price. At least three factors are important here. The first is the degree of competition. In traditional activities this is usually high since there is freedom of entry and a potentially large number of producers. In modern sector activities there may be little competition, because of state monopolies, markets limited in size or protective barriers against foreign competition. A second important factor is the pace (or speed) at which production activities operate. Experience of using new techniques usually leads to increasing efficiency over time. This implies that production lags are shorter and hence that working capital can be reduced. Over time, therefore, the share of profits can be expected to fall for this reason. Finally, profit shares are likely to depend on the attitudes of entrepreneurs. If they require large expected returns to investment, increases in demand are more likely to spill over into imports than to elicit a domestic supply response in terms of increased capacity. Accordingly the share of profits depends on the responsiveness of entrepreneurs to investment opportunities. If they are reluctant to invest, increases in domestic demand result in higher prices, increased imports, or both. Conversely, an animated entrepreneurial class can translate increasing demand into economic growth.

Once investment is determined the system is complete, since investment minus resource depletion generates future factor endowments, which provide the initial conditions for subsequent period analysis. At this point, therefore, we need to consider how the various modules are formally integrated into the over-all framework.

THE FORMAL INCORPORATION OF THE MODULAR FRAMEWORK INTO A SOCIAL ACCOUNTING MATRIX

The modules and their corresponding classification systems in figure 4 can be translated into the social accounting matrix presented in table 4. This table is an extension of the matrix presented in table 2. The new elements, such as the detailed treatment of capital accounts to reflect the initial as well as the revised wealth held as factors of production (which were described in the modules of the preceding section), are incorporated into the new SAM. In fact, table 4 is the informational counterpart of the modular system we have just discussed. Before we proceed, it should be recognised that empirical work today has not progressed very far beyond the quantification of the basic SAM shown in table 2 and in table 6 in the appendix, which is applied to Sri Lanka. [1]

Table 4 involves 14 symmetrical rows and columns. [2] Since a particular row (and the corresponding column) is, in fact, a set of rows defined by the classification used with respect to that aspect of the economy, a very large table would be needed to show all the details. The SAM in table 4 incorporates all the major transformations (such as that from the structure of production to the factorial income distribution, and from the latter to the household income distribution) and relationships contained in the modular framework. A change in any particular element, or account, occurring in this integrated and interconnected system must have repercussions elsewhere.

As in table 2, the rows in table 4 collect together receipts, while columns record the associated expenditures. Hence, each non-zero element of the table is a receipt when read in its row context and an expenditure in its column. In this way, familiar double-entry book-keeping becomes single-entry accounting in the matrix format of table 4.

Row 1 of the table records wants in society. These are wants for food, clothing, housing, education, entertainment, leisure, etc. They are paid for by the expenditures of the different household groups in column 3. Thus at the intersection of row 1 and column 3 we have a table or submatrix showing how much is spent on each want (e.g. calories) by each type of household.

A slightly expanded version of this submatrix is shown as table 5. The rows are different wants, as in table 4. The treatment suggests, however, that these should be defined so as to recognise the distinction between minimum requirements and supernumerary wants. The former, collectively,

---

[1] Subsequent research in Swaziland has covered some of the extensions while work in Malaysia represents further progress.

[2] An additional fifteenth row is defined on a net basis and therefore does not spoil the over-all balance.

constitute the poverty level. Thus minimum requirements may include primary education but exclude secondary schooling, so that the latter is a supernumerary want. This illustrates the subjectivity of a poverty definition and has a bearing on its interpretation as something to which policy ought to pay particular attention. Similarly, basic dietary needs are likely to be a part of minimum requirements, while consumption beyond this level is a supernumerary want.

In table 4, column 3 subdivides households according to their socioeconomic group. Table 5 involves further subdivision within socioeconomic groups between rich and poor. This makes it clear that the poor can satisfy some, but not all, of their basic needs, while the rich, by definition, succeed in meeting basic needs and in addition manage to satisfy some of their supernumerary wants.

One of the immediate consequences of setting out information in the format of table 5 is that the nature of poverty can be discerned. Thus rural poverty's worst symptom may be inadequate diet, while the urban poor's most pressing need may be inadequate housing. The table also allows that minimum requirements may differ between socioeconomic groups because, say, of regional differences between them. Furthermore, the format shows how far there are goods and services available in the society which could be redistributed if this were the best way of achieving desired objectives.

An implication of table 5 is that it questions the extent to which government current expenditure alleviates poverty. This is because "wants" includes items such as basic health services which may, in fact, be provided free by government. As noted earlier, we treat these as imputed incomes and expenditures of the households which receive them. Accordingly, if these services miss those groups who are poorest, they will tend to be satisfying the minimum requirements of the rich (who would otherwise be poorer) rather than contributing directly to poverty alleviation.

Returning to table 4, the totals for the different wants in row 1 record the expenditures incurred in want satisfaction. For each household group these expenditures (or its consumption) are the numerator of its average living standard. The denominator is the poverty level, or the cost which would be incurred if all households in the group satisfied their minimum requirements but no more. Hence the matrix in row 1, column 3 records living standards and poverty within each socioeconomic group. Since we define the main policy objectives in terms of these variables, the purpose of the rest of the table is to ascertain how this particular submatrix is determined and may be altered. In order not to try the patience of our readers further, we relegate the remainder of the technical description of table 4 to the appendix.

Table 4. Final SAM schema (including commodity accounts)

| | | Expenditures | | | | | | | | | | | | | |
| Receipts | | Current accounts | | Domestic institutions | | | Capital accounts | | | | | | Current accounts | | Totals |
		1 Wants	**2** Factors of production	**3** House-holds	**4** Com-panies	**5** Govern-ment	**6** House-holds	**7** Com-panies	**8** Govern-ment	**9** Domestic factor endow-ments	**10** Financial claims	**11** Rest of the world	**12** Rest of the world net excl. imports	**13** Production activities	**14** Commod-ities	
Current accounts	**1** Wants			Want satisfactions												Demand for want and need satisfactions
	2 Factors of production												*Net factor incomes received from abroad*	Value added payments to factors		Incomes of domestic factors of production
	3 Domestic institutions / House-holds		Allocation of labour income to households		Profits distributed to domestic households	*Current actual and imputed transfers to h'holds*										Incomes of the domestic institutions after transfers
	4 Com-panies		Allocation of operating surpluses to companies			*Current transfers to domestic companies*						*Net non-factor incomes received from abroad*				
	5 Govern-ment			*Direct taxes rates*	Company tax rates											
Capital accounts	**6** Domestic institutions / House-holds			Household savings						*Initial wealth held as factors of production*						Revised wealth of the domestic institutions
	7 Com-panies				Undistributed profits after tax						*Initial wealth held as financial claims*					
	8 Govern-ment					Government current account surplus										

44

Receipts	Account		Wants	Factors	Households	Companies	Government	Capital: factor endowments	Capital: financial claims	Capital: foreign claims	Rest of the world	Production activities	Commodities	Totals
Capital accounts	9	Domestic factor endowments		Incomes of domestic factors of production				Revised wealth held as factors of production						Revised factor endowments
	10	Financial claims							Revised wealth as financial claims					Revised financial claims
	11	Rest of the world							Flow of funds *Initial foreign claims on domestic insts.*	Revised foreign claims on domestic institutions	Balance of payments current account deficit			Revised foreign claims
Current accounts	12	Rest of the world imports											imports	Total imports
	13	Production activities											Domestic supplies of commodities	Total revenue
	14	Commodities			H'sehold consump. demand for goods, services		*Govt. demand for goods and services*	*Investment expenditure*			Exports	Raw material purchases		Total commodity demands
	15	Commodity taxes					Net commodity tax receipts						*Indirect tax rates, etc.*	Total revenue
		Totals	Supply of want and need satisfactions	Incomes of domestic factors of production	Total outlay of households	Total outlay of companies	Total outlay of government	Revised factor endowments	Revised financial claims	Revised foreign claims	Total for. exch. receipts *less* imports	Total costs	Total commodity supplies	0

Revised wealth held as factors of production — Revised wealth as financial claims — Revised wealth as domestic institutions

Table 5.   Schematic table of want satisfactions and poverty

Wants			Households		Totals
			Poor	Rich	
			Household types	Household types	
	Minimum requirements	Specific needs	Extent to which the specific needs of the poor are met	Specific needs of the rich	Supplies to meet specific needs
	Supernumerary wants	Specific satisfactions	0	Want satisfactions over and above specific needs	Supplies to meet want satisfactions over and above specific needs

As stated earlier, a recurring theme in our main research is the necessity to consider in a consistent way all the aspects of an economy included in table 4 (and discussed above in this section and in the appendix) to arrive at the determinants of living standards. Within this framework we are greatly concerned with the subclassifications used, since these directly affect the relevance of the calculations which can be made. However, before we turn to the use of table 4 as a way into analysing the behaviour of the economy, some comments on the possibility of using it as a data framework, i.e. of organising numerical facts on this basis, are in order.

It is quite evident from the above discussion that the quantification of table 4 is no trivial matter. However, it is worth noting that, subject to two main exceptions discussed below (i.e. the accounts for wants and the disaggregated household accounts), the details it requires are already included within the United Nations System of National Accounts. [1] Thus, subject to these exceptions, the details are within the system which countries are recommended to adopt and which they have been making great efforts to introduce, and therefore the proposal to direct further efforts towards such a table is not in conflict with other recommendations and is not unrealistic. However, within the broad framework of table 4, we would urge that a new look be taken at the classifications adopted, not least from the point of view of capturing the dualistic nature of production and the fragmentation of labour markets. In several instances, existing practice fails to capture the details which emerge from our study as being crucial. Evidence is difficult to produce, since to show the importance of classifications typically requires going back to primary data sources and reclassifying the results. However, we are able to illustrate our concern for such questions with reference to some input-output calculations undertaken as part of the ILO comprehensive employment strategy mission to the Philippines. [2] These show quite clearly that estimates of the derived demand for labour are very sensitive to the criteria used for defining production activities. While it is unfashionable to be concerned with economic statistics at this level, our analysis indicates that it is extremely important.

The two facets of economic activity introduced in table 4 which are not part of the United Nations System of National Accounts are the accounts for wants and the disaggregated household accounts. The households sector in aggregate is included, of course, while a disaggregated approach and much else that directly relates to our treatment of wants as in table 6 can be

---

[1] United Nations : *A System of National Accounts,* op. cit.

[2] See ILO : *Sharing in development : a programme of employment, equity and growth for the Philippines* (Geneva, 1974), special paper 19 : "Intersectoral linkages and direct and indirect employment effects".

found in the United Nations' complementary System of Social and Demographic Statistics.[1] But we do not want just a *complementary* system : the important point is to integrate questions of poverty and inequality in the aggregate economic framework—or even better to start off with them, as in Gregory King's table (table 1), and to build the other details around them. One of our main recommendations is that work on national data systems can and should be reorganised so that planning can be concerned with poverty and inequality as well as growth.

Because the two United Nations systems are logically consistent, there are no problems at this level in combining the two sets of data. However, our practical experience and that of Altimir[2] indicates clearly the real difficulties which arise when an attempt is made to reconcile information on the distribution of incomes and national accounts. This, then, is an area which calls for more work. Meanwhile, it should be clear, first, that the problems arise in putting the data together, not through any lack of a consistent conceptual cadre ; and second, that these problems of reconciling data to make them consistent can be solved and can result in more accurate estimates at the end of the day.[3] The effort is therefore worth while in that sense.

The problems of filling out table 4 with data present practical difficulties which can be overcome by intelligence and hard work. However, it was indicated at the outset that table 4 is also a framework for the algebraic statement showing how one variable influences another and therefore what determines the numbers in the table. There are no definitive answers to these questions, so that the specific suggestions in our main research must be interpreted only as possible solutions.

In using the SAM framework for operational and policy purposes, we take as exogenous (predetermined) the items which are italicised in table 4 and derive endogenously all the other entries, at both constant and current prices. The algebra is not presented here ; but conclusions rest on it, since our understanding of what might be useful strategy derives in part from the magnitudes of numbers in the table that are likely to be generated as a result of setting the predetermined variables at different levels. Because we have not undertaken actual calculations with real numbers, the conclusions must be tentative. But in building up this framework we have developed some

---

[1] United Nations : *Towards a System of Social and Demographic Statistics,* op. cit.

[2] See O. Altimir : *Income distribution estimates from household surveys and population census in Latin America: an assessment of reliability* (United Nations Economic Commission for Latin America and World Bank Development Research Centre, 1975 ; mimeographed).

[3] Pyatt and Roe, op. cit., discuss informal methods of reconciliation at length. Stone's foreword to that volume sets out a formal method.

sense of the potential results, while simpler specifications have been tested, and economics in general provides guidance. Our conclusions are therefore drawn as extrapolations from known results [1], conditioned by the thinking which has gone into the development of table 4 so far. As such, they are perhaps defensible against prescriptions which are based on less systematic analysis. We turn next to the operational usefulness of our approach—including an analysis of the policy measures which are incorporated in the framework and the outline of the major elements of a development strategy which is suggested by our framework in the light of the objectives.

---

[1] In addition to studies in which we have been directly involved, a model of the Philippines economy by Ng has stimulated our thinking and is reported in our main research (Lu Siong Ng: *An income distribution and employment consistency model of the Philippines* (Ames, Iowa, Iowa State University Department of Economics, 1975)). More recently, Adelman and Robinson have produced a pioneering study of Korea based on a completed model (I. Adelman and S. Robinson: *A wage and price endogenous general equilibrium model of a developing country: factors affecting the distribution of income in the short run* (Washington, DC, World Bank Development Research Centre, 1975 ; mimeographed)), while continuing work by Norton and others in the World Bank is of considerable interest in the treatment of issues similar to those that concern us. In general, all these models can be regarded as more or less special cases of our algebraic treatment.

CONCLUSIONS AND POLICY INFERENCES 3

In retrospect, the three most important contributions which the present approach appears to make to the planning process are : *(a)* the specification of a system for classifying and collecting empirical information in a way appropriate to the planning of the economic and social development process ; *(b)* the construction of the modular conceptual framework which brings out explicitly, in a consistent way, the interdependence between the various parts and variables of the complete system ; and *(c)* the incorporation of policy means and policy objectives in the framework. Potentially, this last contribution permits the identification of appropriate development strategies and, more generally, the simulation of the likely effects of alternative policy packages on the policy objectives within a dynamic setting. All three contributions are highly inter-related.

In Chapter 2 the first two of these contributions (i.e. a modular conceptual framework and a corresponding data system in the form of a social accounting matrix) were formulated. The next step is to describe how the comprehensive SAM framework can be used for policy formulation purposes. Consequently, the present chapter is divided into three sections dealing respectively with the logic of the planning framework and its operational usefulness, the incorporation of policy measures in the framework, and the major elements of a development strategy.

THE LOGIC AND OPERATIONAL USEFULNESS
OF THE PLANNING FRAMEWORK

As table 4 illustrates, the planning framework embraces a number of modules (or subsystems), each with its own set of relationships between variables and corresponding accounts. In turn, the various subsystems are connected by relationships which act as links between one set of variables and another. The SAM provides the appropriate classification, the organisational schema and the underlying algebra for this analytical framework. It was pointed out at the end of the last chapter that in table 4 the values of all endogenous variables can be generated as functions of a set of exogenous variables (shown in italics in the table) representing the initial condition and the policy measures under the control of government.

It is because the initial conditions prevailing in developing countries can differ significantly in terms of such factors as the initial resource endowment and pattern of ownership, the stage of development, the institutional setting and the availability of information that a flexible approach to planning is required. It has already been seen that an important advantage of the modular approach is that it provides much scope for flexibility in the specification of the planning framework.

Given this diversity of settings faced by developing countries and the multiplicity of objectives, such as growth and poverty alleviation, which the planner has to focus upon, a modular consistency approach is likely to be operationally much more useful than an optimisation approach. One major advantage of the consistency framework, which is discussed in more detail subsequently, is that it allows the effects of alternative policy packages on the policy objectives to be traced out in the form of what might be called a "policy navigation table".

Since we are interested in improving the standard of living of individuals and reducing poverty, it is essential to link our performance index (i.e. the geometric mean income) to the basic needs and wants of households, particularly the poor ones. Given a certain society and environment, it is possible to specify minimal requirements for a whole bundle of goods and services [1], and to trace over time the consequences of alternative policies on the growth rate of living standards of different household groups. This process might reveal, inter alia, the undesirable effects of too great an emphasis on equity today, on growth and equity tomorrow—particularly if the former were based mainly on consumption transfers.

Consequently it would be quite meaningless from a planning standpoint

---

[1] Just what these minimal requirements might be is ultimately subjective, corresponding to the fact that poverty is not an absolute concept. But it is real enough and there is a growing number of studies on what is minimal in terms of being just adequate with respect to such items as food, sanitation and shelter. Value judgements are necessary to define what are basic needs, and once these are defined it is implicit that some households will be found to fall short of whatever minima are established. Once these basic needs are specified on a per-adult equivalent basis for the various commodities in the bundle, given the size and composition of the household and the prices (including imputed prices) of the commodities, the total money value needed to maintain the household at, or rather just above, the minimal poverty level of living can be established.

to limit oneself to a static framework and performance measure which focused only on the distribution among individuals of a fixed basket of goods. The fact that growth is not seen as a sole objective of development in no sense implies that it is irrelevant. On the contrary, growth is essential if poverty is to be relieved, especially in many parts of south Asia where the current level of production is simply not sufficient to provide a decent standard of living for everyone, even if total income were to be equally distributed. A trade-off can exist between growth and equality over time. With non-reproducible resources, the problem faced in development planning is to raise living standards to the highest level that can be sustained indefinitely with known technologies.

A major contribution of the planning framework is that the variables in the respective subsystems are broken down in an operationally useful way, while the SAM provides a comprehensive survey of the complete classification scheme and of the transformation, or mapping, between classifications used in the different modules. Thus it can be recalled, following the interdependent sequence represented in figure 3, that households are divided into relatively homogeneous groups according to criteria such as socioeconomic factors, regional considerations and similarities in terms of wealth, income and consumption patterns. Wants are broken down into meaningful categories to reflect food, clothing, shelter and other requirements. Commodities, in turn, are divided into classes permitting an easy mapping between the former as means for satisfying the needs and wants expressed by the household groups.

Next in our sequence, production activities are defined along criteria such as types of commodities produced, form of organisation (i.e. formal, informal) and technology used. In addition, another distinction is made between, first, goods and services which are produced for the market, and second, those which are not and hence lead to imputed (as opposed to actual) income. [1] The production of goods and services requires both intermediate and primary factors of production. The derived demand for the latter generates value added which represents the major source of income accruing to the factors of production. These factors are broken down according to occupational and skill characteristics with regard to labour, according to vintage and other technological factors for capital inputs, and finally, according to agronomic and regional criteria with

---

[1] Clearly, different production activities may give rise to the same commodity—i.e. one production alternative might be in the traditional sector and others in the modern sector so that the matrix linking production activities and commodities would typically not be square. By analogy, the same observation applies to the matrix linking wants and commodities.

respect to land. Hence, the value added returns accruing to these inputs from the production activities generate a factorial income distribution which, finally, can be mapped into the corresponding distribution of income over household groups and other institutions (government and companies). The circular framework in figure 3 is then completed by providing the various categories of households and other institutions with the incomes which determine, in turn, the expenditures pattern of the latter. [1]

One important process incorporated into the planning framework is the determination of income levels and sizes of the various household groups through the operation of factor markets and, particularly, labour markets. Figure 5 illustrates this process. Again, the starting point consists of a given initial resource endowment and set of production activities. In our SAM we distinguish relatively homogenous household groups according to their endowments of resources—for example, possessing specific skills and educational levels (running from totally unskilled labour services to highly professional services), owning, or having tenancy rights to, land of different quality, owning real estate such as dwellings and having ownership or control over capital goods of different vintages. [2] The owners or possessors of factors want to "sell" or exchange the latter for income and consequently represent the supply side of markets for factors of production. Thus workers possess a variety of skills and try to become productively employed ; landowners normally want to see their land used for cultivation or the construction of residential or commercial buildings ; and owners of productive plant capacity and machines are interested in achieving the highest utilisation rates possible.

On the other side of the factor markets, production activities give rise to a derived demand for factors. The detailed modelling or production activities can range from the one extreme of assuming that the output of any given activity requires inputs in constant proportions, to the other extreme of permitting almost perfect substitutability between inputs. The exact form of the production functions (i.e. the extent of substitutability between inputs) is ultimately an empirical question which can only be estimated on a case-by-case basis. At any rate, given the specific form of the production functions, the derived demand for the whole complex of factors follows.

---

[1] Each of the modules of the system depicted in schematic form in figure 3 consists of a set of variables which are functionally related through appropriate equations with some of the latter providing the necessary bridges between the modules. The specific forms and underlying rationales of these relationships were discussed in Chapter 2 and need not be repeated here.

[2] It is clear that in many developing countries the prevailing distribution of assets and skills is extremely uneven.

Figure 5.   Markets for factors of production and determination of income and size
(migration pattern) of household groups

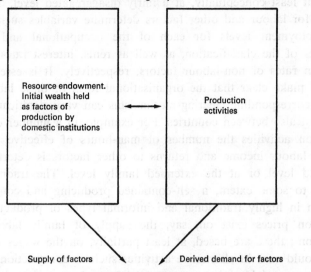

Resource endowment.
Initial wealth held
as factors of
production by
domestic institutions

Production
activities

Supply of factors

Derived demand for factors

Markets for factors of production

Labour markets

Markets for other factors

Determination of wage rates, employment
levels by occupational and skill groups

Determination of land rent, interest rates
and profits accruing to owners of land
and capital and of utilisation rates

Income and size of household groups

Migration pattern

Income

Allocation of households to household
categories defined according to regional,
sociological and wealth criterion

Income determination and distribution
of wants satisfaction by household groups

This confrontation of the supply and demand schedules in our framework occurs, at least conceptually, at a fairly disaggregated level. Thus specific markets for labour and other factors determine variables such as earnings and employment levels for each of the occupational and skill group categories of the classification, as well as rents, interest rates, profits and utilisation rates of non-labour factors, respectively. It is essential, at this stage, to make clear that the organisational form of these labour markets and the corresponding clearing mechanisms can vary significantly not only within but also between countries. For example, in a number of traditional production activities the number of man-hours of effective employment, imputed labour income and returns to other factors is determined at the household level or at the extended family level. The traditional family farm is, to some extent, a self-contained producing and consuming unit. But even in highly traditional and informal types of productive activities reservation prices exist on, say, the supply of family labour for self-production; these are based, at least partially, on the wages which family labour could earn in alternative activities such as construction, or working for hire on a neighbour's or commercial farm. In contrast with the above-described atomistic organisation of production activities, communal or collective systems may yield institutionally determined factor rewards and employment levels. In principle, the proposed framework is flexible enough to model these alternative specifications and institutional settings.

If we return to figure 5 it can be seen that, once the utilisation rates (effective employment levels) and the prices of the different types of factor have been derived, an additional mapping is necessary to obtain the corresponding incomes accruing to the specific household categories and the number of households in each category. In other words, this process allocates factorial income to the household groups and helps to explain the migration pattern between the latter. Hence, estimates of the changes in the standards of living and of the sizes of these groups over time are generated within the framework in an internally consistent way. [1]

This last process illustrates one way in which our framework can be used to model the dynamics of development and not simply the static interdependence between variables and subsystems. Another process which is clearly dynamic is that which explains asset formation and changes in the endowment factors of production enjoyed by different households.

---

[1] The above analysis abstracts from the impact of policy measures which are discussed in the following sections. It is clear that the incorporation of transfers, subsidies and government services benefiting certain groups alters the resulting distribution of income among, and the sizes of, the household categories.

Figure 6 illustrates schematically the process of asset formation and, more specifically, the role of savings and investment. At any given point in time, say year *t*, an economy starts with a given initial distribution of resource endowment across households and other institutions, in terms of educational and skill levels, ownership or possession of land, property and capital goods and financial claims. Similarly, the structure of production is fixed in terms of a set of production activities. The combination of initial wealth and the structure of production (shown at the top of figure 6) generates flows of value added which accrue to the owners of resources. Hence, as was shown previously, the various household groups receive income from such sources as wages and imputed labour income, rent from land and from other property (e.g. imputed housing rent), interest and profits. Similarly, companies and government enjoy revenues which originate in the production sphere.

This allocation of factorial income to the domestic institutions (properly modified to reflect transfers, subsidies and the imputed value of public goods and services benefiting different groups as well as taxes paid by these groups) yields the current values of the policy objectives, i.e. the levels of employment and utilisation rates of the factors, the magnitude of GNP and the standards of living of the different classes of household. These current objectives are shown in the circles which appear on the right-hand side of figure 6. (Incidentally, it should be noted that, depending on the type of political and economic system which prevails, the allocation of factor income to companies might instead accrue to state enterprises and thus be depicted with the other sources of government revenue in a single sphere.)

Each of the three categories of institution referred to above generates surplus funds over and above present consumption, which take the form, respectively, of household savings, undistributed profits after taxes and current government surplus. Together these sources of savings provide the pool for net investment. [1] Given the inadequacies of capital markets and of the financial intermediation process, a substantial degree of compartmentalisation exists within groups of institutions with respect to the channelling of savings into investment. For example, traditional households in agriculture typically have to finance investment out of their own savings

---

[1] In this analysis we have abstracted from the rest of the world. In fact, it is clear that government, companies and even, in some cases, households can borrow abroad. This means that an additional part of net investment (not shown in figure 6) consists of net foreign investment. The availability of foreign private investment and aid can be an important potential source of capital as was discussed in Chapter 2. Again, it should be noted that figure 6 is a subset of figure 4.

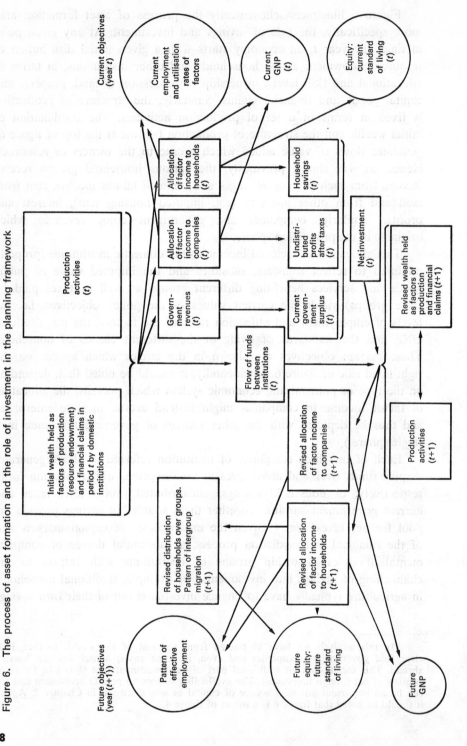

Figure 6. The process of asset formation and the role of investment in the planning framework

since they cannot borrow in the capital markets. Similarly, other relatively disfavoured groups such as households in the informal urban sector normally have to rely on their own savings to obtain the necessary working capital for their artisanal and workshop activities. This segmentation in the savings-cum-investment process helps to explain why in these households most savings and investment decisions tend to be simultaneous.[1] This simultaneity implies that the total pool of savings involved is not available to finance any investment ; investment projects undertaken by certain types of household are limited by the savings generated by these same households.

Returning to figure 6, it can be seen that, in addition to net investment, changes in financial claims between groups (through the financial inter-mediation and flow of funds process) give rise in year $(t + 1)$ to *(a)* a revised resource endowment and pattern of factor ownership by the different institutions, and more particularly the various household groups ; and *(b)* a new complex of production activities. More specifically, the asset position of any group in society can be affected only through investment benefiting this group, which must itself be financed by the savings of that group or by loans or grants to it. But if loans have collateral as a prerequisite, it follows that the assets of the poor cannot begin to increase until they themselves start to save or until government redistributes assets through structural changes such as educational and land reforms.

A major advantage of the present planning framework and data system is that it captures the segmented nature of the savings-cum-investment process and its impact on the revised distribution of wealth among households and other institutions. The revised wealth distribution, in turn, is likely to influence the structure of production activities by changing the output mix (some activities becoming more important than others) and by inducing new activities, in at least some instances. A revised endowment of resources in favour of certain groups of households, such as an agrarian reform providing land to previously landless workers or a large-scale public investment programme in traditional agriculture (say, in irrigation), may induce the farmers to adopt somewhat different technologies. In the land distribution case, a shift from mechanised technologies to more labour-intensive intermediate technologies might occur in line with the reduction in the average size of the farm and the revised distribution of value added

---

[1] For instance, housing facilities are built on a do-it-yourself basis : any time and money available over and above the need to provide basic necessities may be used to acquire materials and construct new or improved dwellings. Similarly, traditional farmers engage in a variety of accretionary activities which require simultaneous savings and investment decisions, such as land improvement and levelling, the digging of small irrigation canals and the setting-aside of seed from the present crop to grow the next crop.

(land rent accruing now to the new (small) landlords instead of accruing to the previous (large) landlords). In the other example above, an irrigation project in traditional agriculture is likely to encourage the adoption of high-yielding "green revolution" types of technology (at least for cereals) in place of almost completely labour-intensive techniques. This interrelationship between a revised resource endowment and the structure of production is very important from a policy standpoint and is elaborated upon in the next section.

The next step in the asset formation process is the revised allocation of factor income to households and other institutions resulting from the revised wealth distribution and structure of production, shown graphically in figure 6 by the arrows moving from south to west. In this fashion, the magnitudes of future policy objectives (in year $(t + 1)$) are determined. [1] Hence the future GNP level, employment pattern and distribution of income among household groups are derived from and can be compared with the values of these same objectives in the current period. Our planning framework lends itself particularly well to the analysis of the trade-offs which might exist between present and future equity. The dynamic process described above illustrates clearly the conflicts which can arise between alternative development paths. An essential point, in this context, is not just that larger aggregate savings today might generate a higher aggregate growth rate of output, but that the *pattern* of savings, as between household groups and institutions, and structural changes in the initial resource endowment may be more important determinants of future equity and growth. It is not just the lack of aggregate savings which precludes improvements in the standards of living of the poor but rather the amount of specific savings generated by them and the unfavourable initial resource endowment which they face.

THE INCORPORATION OF POLICY MEASURES IN THE FRAMEWORK

It is clear that the interdependent system described in the previous section will be affected by changes or shocks occurring in any of the modules. Some of these shocks are exogenous, in the sense that they are outside the control of the policy maker, while others are clearly under government control. The essence of development planning is to design a strategy which is appropriate in the light of the policy objectives. This section is devoted to a review and analysis of the major policy measures

---

[1] These future policy objectives appear on the extreme left-hand side of figure 6.

incorporated in the framework, while the next section concentrates on identifying the major elements of a development strategy.

It was seen in the last section that the two essential initial determinants of the development process over time are the structure of production, which is modelled as a set of activities, and the pattern of ownership of the factors in the base period. Consequently a distinction should be made between the policy measures which are available to a government within a *given* institutional structure and pattern of ownership of resources and those which, if undertaken, affect the latter directly and thereby alter the underlying structure of the economy. The first class of policy means includes policy instruments in Tinbergen's nomenclature, i.e. marginal or incremental quantitative changes in policies *within* an economic and social structure. In contrast, structural changes and policy reforms alter directly the distribution of resources and the wealth pattern among different groups in society in the planning period. This distinction between sets of policy means is useful when considering the different approaches to economic and social development, ranging from a reliance on a more "conservative" package of policy measures to a more "radical" one. [1]

In our framework the effects of a given package of policy measures on the set of policy objectives can be simulated. This resulting set represents what might be called the feasible policy space. By expanding the package of policy measures the feasible policy space is similarly expanded. Thus more desirable values of all, or most, objectives could result from a more ambitious package of policy means which would reduce, or eliminate altogether, a previous trade-off between equity and growth. [2] This expansion of the policy space is a much more important phenomenon in our framework than the specification of an objective function *per se*. Clearly, it is more relevant to identify whether a certain path may yield both more growth and equity over time than alternative ones, rather than to apply a radical preference function to a restricted set of policy measures.

In the next section, which is devoted to outlining the major elements of a broadly based and distributionally oriented development strategy, an attempt will be made to identify the appropriate package or packages of

---

[1] Three such approaches can be identified: *(a)* the incremental approach; *(b)* the interventionist approach; and *(c)* the radical-reformist approach. Although these approaches are by no means mutually exclusive (if anything they can often complement one another), there is a tendency for many countries to concentrate more on one approach (sets of policy means), depending on their preference function and political orientation.

[2] In fact, the new policy feasibility frontier yields new trade-offs between objectives but at a preferred level for all objectives, compared with the previous frontier. This question was discussed at the end of Chapter 1.

the different types of policy measure listed below. In that section, the joint and reinforcing effect of a package of policy measures embracing a development strategy is analysed. Meanwhile, in the present section an attempt is made to identify in which modules of the system specific policy measures are incorporated and to analyse, briefly, the individual impact of each measure on the over-all planning system.

The policy measures appearing in the planning framework may be classified as follows :

1. *Policy instruments* (operating within a given pattern of ownership of factors) :

    (a) "fine-tuning" instruments :

        (i) use of "efficiency" prices reflecting opportunity costs of resources in the light of preference function. Commodity tax and subsidy rates. Removal of artificial price distortions. Public utility pricing ;

        (ii) removal of discriminatory market imperfections ;

        (iii) appropriate exchange rate and commercial policies ;

    (b) fiscal instruments and transfers :

        (i) direct taxes on households and companies ;

        (ii) actual and imputed public transfers to households ;

        (iii) transfers to companies ;

    (c) monetary and credit policy ;

    (d) public investment and choice of projects (including projects financed by foreign assistance).

2. *Structural changes and policy reforms* (assuming changes in the pattern of ownership of factors) :

    (a) land reform ;

    (b) changes in ownership of other physical capital assets ;

    (c) educational reforms.

As a very broad generalisation it could be argued that countries emphasising economic growth and production in the modern sector are more likely to rely on the incremental, "fine-tuning" price-incentive approach while maintaining the status quo in the economic and social structure. At the other extreme, governments placing a very high relative welfare weight on achieving a relatively even income distribution in the near future are more likely to undertake reforms in the distribution of assets. Figure 7 reproduces the previously discussed causal interdependence between the modules of the planning framework (see figure 3) in the inner circle—or rather pentagon—while indicating on the outer circle the major policy measures which can be formally incorporated into that framework and their approximate "points of entry" into the over-all system.

Policy instruments

The "fine-tuning" instruments embrace the use of an appropriate price system (including commodity tax and subsidy rates), the removal of market imperfections and appropriate exchange rate and commercial policies. Since we are dealing with an interdependent system, the impact of these measures will be felt in many parts of it, but probably the most noticeable impact will be on the structure of production through resulting changes in the output mix between production activities and the input mix within activities.

Thus the removal of artificial price distortions, such as credit sub-sidisation favouring large entrepreneurs and farmers and an overvalued exchange rate, tend to lower the cost of capital below the value of its marginal value product ; on the other hand, the existence of such factors as minimum wage legislation and various social charges which have to be borne by employers tends to raise the cost of labour above its marginal contribution to output. In the present framework the specification of production activities allows us to measure the impact of the removal, or reduction, of price distortions (i.e. changes in relative input prices) on the demand for inputs. This quantitative impact on the magnitude of the substitution elasticities would, in the capital-labour case, reflect the relative increase in employment resulting from a relative fall in wages or in the wage/rental ratio.

The removal of such price distortions may be desirable in the sense that it may lead to increased employment. Government can use the whole gamut of commodity tax and subsidy rates to affect relative input and output prices and thereby to influence effective demand. In turn, changes in the demand pattern resulting from the differential effects of specific taxes and subsidies lead to corresponding changes in the mix of production activities (see figure 7). Ultimately the incomes accruing to different household groups are altered.

At the same time, subsidies can be used directly to provide basic commodities such as food or services to poor households at reduced prices.

Government consumption

Public investment (choice of projects)

Distribution of income over households and other institutions

Direct taxes on households and companies

Current transfers to domestic companies

Government actual and imputed transfers to households

Factors of production, GNP, factorial income distribution

Wants, basic needs

Household expenditures on wants

Investment expenditures and government consumption

Exports, imports and balance of payments

Rate of exchange, commercial policy

Commodity expenditures and final demand

Commodity tax and subsidy rates

Structural changes and reforms in initial resource endowment

Production activities

Monetary and credit policy

Price policy, increased competition

Figure 7. Major policy measures and their incorporation in the planning framework

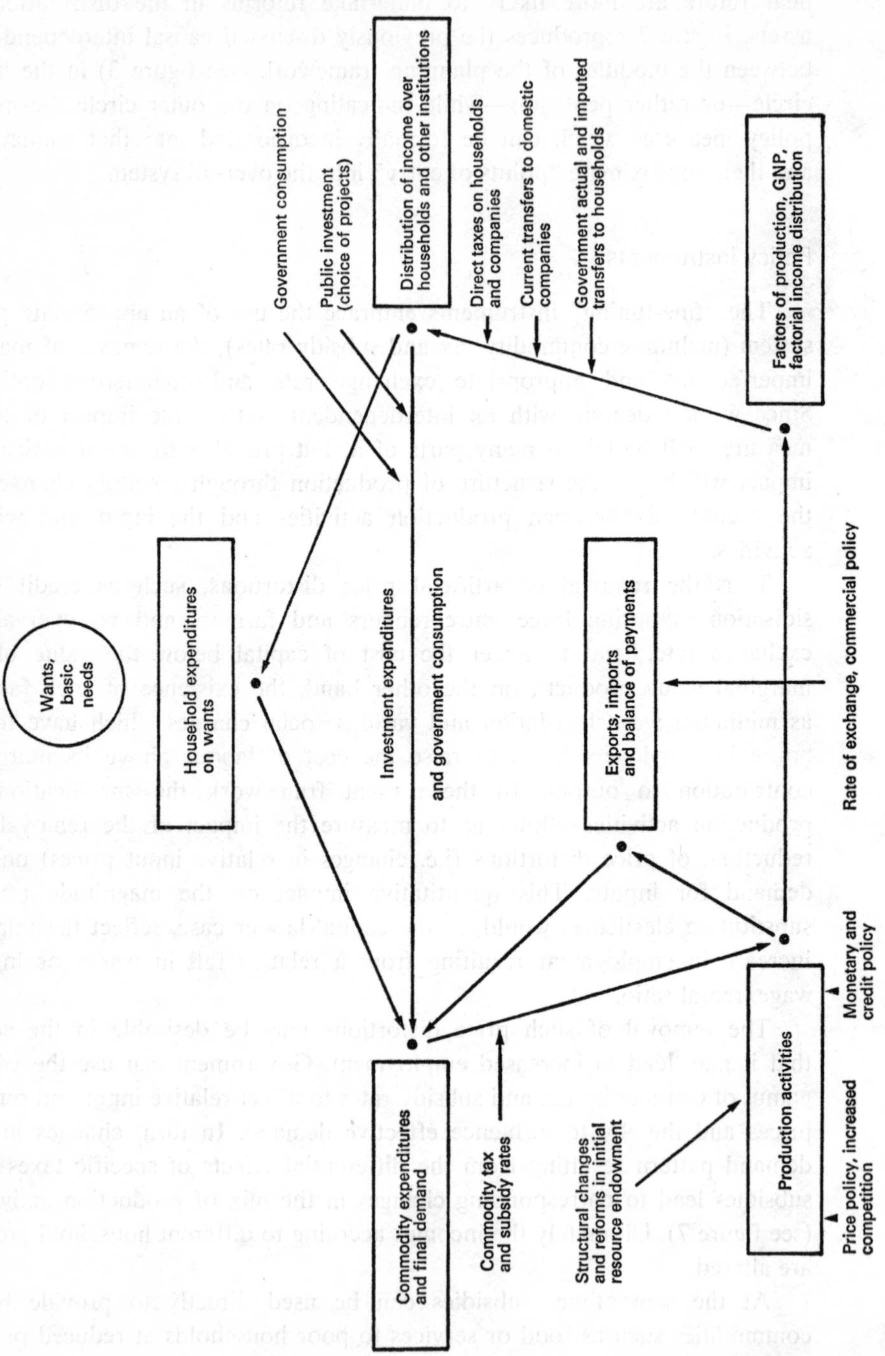

It is even possible to visualise a differential subsidy-cum-indirect-tax scheme which would operate progressively by recapturing from the rich the subsidies required to provide certain goods and services below cost to the poor.

It should be clear, in general, that an appropriate use of such taxes and subsidies, as well as appropriate pricing policies for state and regulated enterprises, can help to push the feasible policy space outward. Table 4, discussed in Chapter 2, permits us to follow the effects of changes in these instruments on the whole SAM system.

The formulation of production activities adopted in the framework is sufficiently flexible to model both extremes of fixed proportions and perfect substitutability between inputs. In the former case, changes in relative input prices would mean a shift from one production activity to another, e.g. from wheat produced under a mechanised technology to wheat produced under an intermediate technology. In the second case, the extent of the substitutability between inputs would be built directly into each production activity and the input requirements would vary depending on the prices. Hence changes in relative output prices would lead to a revised demand for factors and thereby affect the factorial and ultimately the household income distribution and feed back through the expenditure subsystem into a given effective demand for the output of production activities. In this fashion, through the interdependence of the system, changes in the relative prices of commodities are translated into a new demand pattern.

Even though the sensitivity of factor demand to changes in input prices is probably limited on technological grounds, there are some sectors (such as agriculture) in which the choice of techniques is sufficiently wide to make it possible for an appropriate price system combined with other measures to be an effective instrument in employment creation and poverty reduction. [1]

A second type of "fine-tuning" instrument consists of the elimination or reduction of existing market imperfections in both the input and the output markets. The classical or neoclassical remedy for reducing monopolistic or monopsonistic imperfections is to increase competition through such means as antitrust legislation and the prohibition of discriminatory pricing. In fact, there is strong evidence that a large number of developing countries instituted commercial policies and other measures which interfered with competitive conditions. Thus the various instruments used to protect domestic industries from foreign competition in the strategy of industrial-

---

[1] In addition, an appropriate price system may be an essential inducement to the design of appropriate technology.

isation through import substitution (such as licensing schemes, high protective tariffs and multiple exchange rates) provided a large rent element to these protected industries. In general, there is empirical evidence that the over-all effect of the import substitution phase was *(a)* to accentuate the gap between the modern and the traditional sectors ; *(b)* to discriminate against agriculture ; and *(c)* to encourage, in many cases, the adoption of inappropriate technologies. Here again, the distinction between import and domestic productive activities in our production subsystem permits us to measure both the efficiency cost of such policies and whether they might have contributed to unemployment and poverty by discriminating against traditional agricultural and urban informal activities.

In conclusion, the "fine-tuning" instruments can perhaps best be incorporated in our framework by first analysing their direct impact on the production subsystem, through changes in the composition of output (as between production activities) and in the demand for inputs. In turn, the effects of these changes can be traced, either sequentially or interdependently, on the various subsystems of our planning framework as illustrated in figure 7.

A second type of policy instrument consists of the various fiscal instruments and transfers. The following measures are explicitly incorporated in our planning framework : direct taxes on households and companies ; actual and imputed public transfers to households ; and transfers to companies. These three fiscal instruments influence and modify the mapping from the factorial income distribution to the distribution of income over households and other institutions, as can be seen in figure 7. It is clear that government can use these measures to redistribute income towards those groups it wants to favour and away from other groups. Conceptually, direct taxes and money transfers can be modelled reasonably easily in our framework. However, to do so with commodities or services that may be provided free to some households, such as education and health services, is more difficult. Since households have wants with respect to such items, they will take advantage of them in practice. However, such items are rarely absolutely free (schoolbooks may have to be bought, and there may be a loss of earnings in sending children to school), so that the opportunity cost to the household will rarely be zero. It is unlikely that such costs on the demand side will match the opportunity cost (in terms of scarce resources) of supplying free education or other public services to a limited fraction of the population. Indeed, the whole purpose of such services is to improve the welfare of certain groups, such as poor households ; consequently these unpaid benefits need to be accounted for as an imputed income and expenditure of the households which enjoy these services.

In the present framework, the real living standards of households are adjusted by imputing benefits from free or subsidised government services to the benefiting groups, as well as by imputing the costs in terms of market prices deviating from production opportunity costs developing from policies such as the imposition of direct taxes on other groups.

Even though, in principle, fiscal instruments can have a significant redistributional impact in the short term, it is not unusual in practice to observe that they often tend to increase inequalities rather than to reduce them. [1] The fact that fiscal instruments can be incorporated in the present framework makes it possible to analyse their effects on the present and future living standards of different household groups. In this connection it will be seen in the next section that these instruments, while potentially capable of reducing income inequalities between households, have only a very indirect effect on the productive capacity and resource endowment of the poor groups. For example, higher-quality subsidised education and medical services to the rural poor may over time upgrade their skill levels and thereby their educational endowment.

Monetary and credit policy can play some part in reducing disparities in living levels and acting as a catalyst by encouraging the output growth of traditional and informal activities. Typically, monetary and credit instruments tend to favour enterprises and groups in the modern sector rather than those in the traditional or informal sectors. A notable example of discrimination against the latter sectors is the very limited availability of credit to small farmers and informal workers as opposed to its easy availability to large commercial farmers and entrepreneurs in modern activities. Thus a reduction of the difference between the effective interest rate applying to those two groups might encourage the adoption of somewhat more productive technologies which would, in turn, contribute to higher output and income levels accruing to these poor households. There is a great need for credit and savings institutions catering for traditional and informal activities, so as to eliminate the usurious charges which often prevail in these sectors.

A final type of policy instrument which is formally incorporated in the consistency framework is the allocation of public investment to projects and sectors. It is clear that the allocation of public investment can have a significant effect on the composition of output by sector or by activity. Both capital/output and capital/labour ratios differ substantially between activities, particularly "traditional" and "modern" activities. A set of projects

---

[1] Thus, for example, the quality of educational services in the traditional rural areas tends to be much lower than in more prosperous city districts.

enhancing the productive capacity of traditional agriculture (such as the building of irrigation works, farm-to-market roads and other "mini-infrastructure" activities) results in drastically different outputs, employment and distributional effects from those that the same total investment would give if expended on building a steel mill or a modern petrochemical plant. In essence, the process of selecting public projects and deciding on a given sectoral allocation of public investment is a crucial incremental instrument available to the policy maker. By altering the destination of public investment the output mix can be changed, thus affecting the required complementary levels of the various labour skill groups and intermediate inputs. Any initial increase in sectoral output resulting from new investment projects (or sets of projects) will require additional intermediate inputs from other sectors. In turn, the resulting increased production of these supplying sectors can only occur—in the absence of excess capacity at the outset —through additional investment which will augment the productive capacity. Furthermore, aggregate income rises throughout this process, generating additional demand which can be satisfied only through still more increments to the stock of capital over time.

Even though the treatment of public investment in our framework could not simulate all these indirect effects, it does provide an approximation to a general equilibrium approach to investment projects. [1] One practical difficulty should be mentioned regarding the use of the analytical framework to estimate the output, employment and distributional effects of given public investment allocations, namely that projects or sets of projects may not fall clearly into any given production activity. Thus a set of infrastructure projects to increase the productivity of traditional agriculture may affect the yield of various crops (and hence various activities) differentially. The building of a road or harbour may similarly cut across a series of activities. The limited degree of overlap between some (large) public projects and the activities whose output is increased as a result means that in a number of cases the distribution of this investment by activity (or sector) of destination has to be imputed. [2] An additional problem in the use of public investment as an instrument to affect output and income distribution is its thoroughly incremental (not to say marginal) nature. Indeed, in the section below dealing with the major elements of

---

[1] More specifically, we used in our framework a "semi-input-output" method which assumes that the capital goods required to supply the second and further rounds of inputs will be made available through increased imports or reduced exports with respect to traded goods. It is only with respect to sectors which produce non-traded goods that the necessary increased capacity has to be supplied from domestic sources.

[2] The multilevel specification of production activities in our framework helps to resolve this problem.

a development strategy a simple numerical example will be used to clarify this point.

Structural changes and reforms

The next set of policy measures which can be incorporated into our framework is made up of structural changes and policy reforms directly modifying the initial pattern of ownership (or control) of resources, i.e. land and natural resources, fixed capital and skills. Thus, unlike the policy instruments reviewed previously, reforms directly affect the resource endowment of households and other institutions in the current planning period.

Land tends to be unevenly distributed in many parts of the developing world. There are at least three major reasons why an uneven land distribution generates an uneven income distribution and vice versa : *(a)* the return to land accrues to the large landholders in the form of rent, whereas in the case of the more equal farm size distribution (small-scale agriculture) rental income can usually not be distinguished from labour income and accrues to the smallholder ; *(b)* there is a substantial amount of empirical evidence indicating that constant returns to scale prevail in agriculture and that large estates tend to underutilise the available land resources, so that, as a consequence, labour intensity per unit of land is negatively correlated with the size of the land holding [1] ; *(c)* the institutional and political structure which accompanies a bimodal land distribution tends to favour the large farmers through their easier access to credit and extension services, the greater availability of public investment infrastructure projects, a distorted price system and a degree of monopolistic or monopsonistic power.

These three reasons are in fact processes which can be modelled in the consistency framework. First, the sectoral income distribution resulting from production on large holdings maps into a more uneven personal income distribution than that generated by a land distribution favouring small-scale agriculture. The causes of this differential effect are partially technological and partially intrinsic to the pattern of ownership itself. The large farmers are likely to use more capital-intensive techniques (or at least methods using a higher proportion of intermediate inputs) than small farmers. This phenomenon is reflected in a reduced share of value added

---

[1] In a recent detailed empirical study based on a number of countries, Berry and Cline provide strong supporting evidence for these relationships. See R. A. Berry and W. R. Cline : *Farm size, factor productivity and technical change in developing countries* (Washington, DC, World Bank, 1976 ; mimeographed).

in gross output and a smaller share of labour income relative to non-labour income, to the extent that mechanised techniques are used. Furthermore, as was mentioned in *(a)* above, the rent income *per se* is received by a few landlords or large farmers in the uneven land distribution case and is spread among a large number of small farmers (becoming almost indistinguishable from labour income in traditional agriculture) in the alternative case of an even size distribution of holdings. The combined effect of these forces is a high degree of concentration in the personal income distribution in the former case and a low degree in the latter. This first process is a good example of the inter-relationship in our framework between the initial resource endowment and the choice of technology which, in turn, is translated into a new mix of production activities or, at least, a changed derived demand for factors of production.

The second factor above signifies that land redistribution resulting in smaller average holdings need not necessarily reduce output. Indeed, if constant returns to scale predominate in agriculture, a breakdown of large land units into smaller ones would yield exactly the same total output, as long as the volume of all inputs remains constant. In fact, it is very likely that more labour input per acre is applied to land on small units than on larger holdings. Hence, in theory (and under constant returns to scale, no change in technology and the application of more labour inputs), total production should rise consequent to land redistribution. In reality, as was just mentioned, the technology used by the small farmers may be different from that used by the large farmers. Institutions which previously were favouring the large farmers may not be adapted immediately to solve the needs of smallholders—for example, in the areas of credit and extension services. Finally, the level of certain types of input such as the quality of management may actually decline as a consequence of a land reform. For all these reasons, one cannot necessarily expect a rise in total production to go hand in hand with land redistribution. There might even exist a trade-off between the output objective *per se* and a more equal income distribution over a transitional period. We return to this question in the next section, where it is argued that a land redistribution scheme by itself (i.e. not accompanied by an appropriate set of institutional changes) may be doomed to failure as a structural policy measure conducive to a broadly based process of economic and social development.

This last point leads us directly to the third reason why an uneven land distribution generates an uneven income distribution and vice versa. Institutional changes and policy measures favourable to small farmers are an essential complement to a land redistribution if the dual goals of rural equity and growth are to be achieved.

In summary, our macroeconomic consistency framework makes it possible to analyse quantitatively the direct and indirect effects of changes in the initial endowment of land and of the inter-relationship between the latter and the whole set of production activities.

A second type of structural change which can be modelled in our framework refers to the pattern of ownership of capital and the operation of capital markets. Many developing countries are characterised by a great concentration of wealth and capital assets, on the one hand, and the almost complete absence of capital markets, on the other. Since increased production is normally financed from retained earnings—often in unincorporated family firms—or from direct investment from abroad, the environment is not conducive to the development of an active capital market from the demand for capital side. On the other hand, the lack of financial intermediaries to help to channel savings into investment means that the supply of capital and loanable funds is often institutionally short-circuited as well.

Here, as in the case of land, the inter-relationship between the pattern of ownership of capital assets and the structure of production can be modelled in the framework. Thus the uneven endowment of capital both influences and is influenced by an institutional and technological structure favouring "modernisation", the adoption of foreign advanced techniques and, in general, the continuation of economic dualism. The fact that production in many modern activities is relatively capital intensive and that the ownership of capital is highly concentrated results in limited labour absorption and a skewed personal distribution of non-labour (profit) income which, in turn, is a major reason why an over-all household income distribution may be uneven. A specific measure which can be simulated within the framework is the institution of new financial intermediaries which would increase the transfer of funds between sectors and household groups. It will be seen in the next section that such a step could have important consequences.

In general, some widening of the ownership of capital assets and of access to capital funds can be a key tool in encouraging the adoption of new and more productive technologies by poor household groups, whether in agriculture or in the urban informal sector, and thereby in improving their standard of living over time.

Education and skill formation represent a form of human capital formation. As the productivity of a worker is increased with the amount of capital goods available to him or her, an individual's productivity normally rises with his or her level of education and skills. Consequently any changes in the educational system benefiting the poor, such as a greater emphasis on higher-quality and more relevant primary education than on higher education, and on informal and recurrent education in the rural areas rather than on formal education in the urban areas, should result in a larger share of factorial income accruing to these groups. The issue is less often one of increasing public expenditures on education than one of altering the composition of these expenditures. It has been well documented that the prevailing uneven distribution of human capital is reflected in many developing countries in large differentials in the wages, salaries and labour incomes of the self-employed received by the various household groups.

It might be noted that the treatment and classification of skill and educational groups in the consistency framework and the corresponding SAM can be made to reflect either of the two main theories which relate income distribution to education, i.e. the human capital theory and the labour market segmentation theory. The former postulates that the level and distribution of earnings is directly influenced by the amount of schooling or education received by individuals. In contrast, the labour market segmentation school divides the labour markets into relatively homogeneous types of job, each with distinct characteristics regarding hiring and advancement, working conditions and wage levels and each with different groups to fill these jobs. [1] The approach which we favour is eclectic in the sense that a certain degree of segmentation between labour markets and socioeconomic groups is accepted, together with the role which education can play in facilitating upward mobility between occupations and socioeconomic groups.

In general, it is clear that the policy maker can alter the supply of different skills through the educational system. In this fashion the wage structure can be affected over time and differentials between occupations and jobs can be reduced. Furthermore, to a large extent government controls the wage rates and salaries paid in public sector activities. Often these rates are set at levels which encourage "educated unemployment", particularly on the part of the young—i.e. waiting until a job in the bureaucracy becomes available rather than accepting a lower paid and less secure job in the private sector. High remunerations in public sector activities contribute to a skewed personal income distribution and might, furthermore, discourage the creation of an entrepreneurial group.

---

[1] Those favouring the human capital approach see the incomes of individuals as causally influenced by education, whereas those favouring the latter approach see only a correlation between these two variables, which is explained by the fact that education may simply be the "union card", or the screening device, required to enter a given labour market.

MAJOR ELEMENTS OF A DEVELOPMENT STRATEGY

Now that we have reviewed the major policy measures incorporated in the planning framework and data system, it might be desirable to outline the major elements of a distributionally oriented development strategy.

However, before embarking on the identification of the major elements of such a strategy, some important observations should be made with regard to the operational usefulness of the framework and the corresponding data system.

First, it should be clear by now that a major advantage of the social accounting matrix is that it provides a systematic and consistent way of identifying the initial conditions which exist in an economy. Obviously, an appropriate and thorough specification of the initial conditions yields a policy diagnosis and foundations upon which the development strategy can be built. Different initial conditions will require different packages of policy measures even where the objective function is similar.

The social accounting matrix also suggests the kind of data needed for policy formulation and the form in which this information might be presented. Hence the complete classification scheme, underlying the various subsystems of the SAM, provides guidelines to statistical offices regarding the specific type of information that policy makers seek. In turn, the guidelines may be of great assistance to statistical offices in the process of designing surveys and censuses and in gathering and tabulating other types of information.

A second major advantage of our framework is that it allows a certain amount of policy simulation. The comprehensive dynamic effects of alternative packages of policy measures on the whole system generate what might be called the policy feasibility space defined in terms of the set of objectives. A restrictive package of policy means maps into a limited policy feasibility space and vice versa. [1] Hence our approach to planning does not require the explicit specification of an objective function as such. A comparison of alternative paths over time of the major policy objective provides, as it were, a set of policy navigation tables from which a choice can be made. On the other hand, the specification of an explicit objective function, such as the one we proposed, makes the task of selecting the appropriate strategy simpler. The point to underline, however, is that the present approach to planning does not depend on a narrow specification of the objective function. It is quite flexible, not only in modelling very different initial conditions but also in making it possible to trace through

---

[1] See our analysis of this question at the end of Chapter 1.

the system the effects of different sets of policy without having to specify the preference function *ex ante*.

Furthermore, the framework seems applicable to countries following very different economic and political systems, from an essentially mixed economy to a controlled economy. The only qualification is that government should have an interest in exploring the fulfilment of basic needs over time. The framework can to a limited extent estimate the trade-off between an improvement in the current standard of living of the different household groups and future improvements. In a more general sense, the policy navigation tables illustrate quantitatively the growth paths in the living standards of the various household groups. By revealing to the policy maker the extent to which basic needs can be fulfilled over time, the ultimate choice will depend, of course, on the distributional time preference of the former.

We return now to the outline of the major elements of an appropriate development strategy. The term "appropriate" is, of course, relevant only in the context of a given preference or objective function. Even though it is not necessary to adopt the specific objective function proposed in the framework, it is assumed that the planner is concerned with the satisfaction of basic needs over time. Though the strategy is distributionally oriented, growth is an integral part of it since, without growth, standards of living could not keep on rising over time.

The elements of the development strategy outlined in what follows can be expressed only in a fairly general form since specific measures can be recommended only in the light of the initial conditions which prevail in the country under consideration.

A useful starting point in identifying the main features of the development strategy is to recognise the endemic nature of dualism in large parts of the developing world. Perhaps the two most important dimensions of dualism are regional and technological. The first dimension would distinguish between urban and rural areas and the second dimension between modern, capital-intensive technologies and forms of organisation, on the one hand, and traditional, labour-intensive ones, on the other. Even though there is some overlap between these dimensions they certainly do not coincide. Modern, usually industrial activities tend to be concentrated in the urban areas while traditional agriculture is, of course, located in the rural areas. However, it is true that the informal sector is centred on the cities while, in many countries, a large subsector of agriculture consists of commercial, often export-oriented crops produced with mechanised techniques. [1] The

---

[1] Hence it might be more appropriate to talk about a dual-dual structure as being characteristic of developing countries rather than just a dual structure as such.

rationale for the above two-way distinction is based on the fact that the bulk of poverty is concentrated in the rural areas and associated with the use of traditional, informal technologies, organisational forms and institutions. If poverty is to be eradicated, more resources will have to be directed towards traditional agriculture and informal urban activities through a combination of "incremental"-type policy instruments and structural changes and reforms which directly alter the resource endowment of the household groups in these sectors. Consequently we shall concentrate in what follows, first, on describing the major elements of an appropriate rural-agricultural strategy, and second, on the type of policy package which might be appropriate in the urban, non-agricultural activities. Essentially, the former requires a reduction in the dualism which might exist not only between the traditional small-scale subsector and the commercialised large-scale subsector in agriculture but also between agriculture and industry.

At this stage it is relevant to focus on possible typologies of countries in the light of their initial resource endowment. Bell and Duloy[1] have suggested a typology which appears appropriate in the present context. It is based on three criteria : *(a)* the share of population and GNP per head in rural and urban areas ; *(b)* the availability of land ; and *(c)* the degree of concentration of land ownership. This typology gives rise to eight possible cases of which there are three archetypes : "Latin America", "South Asia" and "Africa". For each of these different development strategies are recommended, depending on the initial conditions.

Briefly, the "Latin America" setting is characterised by a relative abundance of land and an extreme concentration of ownership. The worst of the rural poverty problem can be overcome by an effective land reform which will, furthermore, reduce rural-urban migration and alleviate somewhat the extent of future urban poverty.

The "South Asia" case hinges on demographic pressures on scarce land resources and a relatively high proportion of population in rural areas. These two elements combine to cause widespread and persistent poverty. Given these conditions the comparative advantage of these countries in the long term appears to lie outside agriculture, and long-term development strategy must concentrate on labour-intensive industrialisation. At the same time, according to Bell and Duloy[2], a "holding operation" in the rural areas is recommended for at least two or three decades. Such a strategy should "provide relief as rapidly as possible to the most

---

[1] C. L. G. Bell and J. H. Duloy : "Formulating a strategy", in Chenery *et al.*, op. cit.

[2] ibid., pp. 102-103.

disadvantaged sections of the rural population, and ... should ... not lock the economy into rural institutions which are inimical to future growth".

Finally, for tropical "Africa" a rural-based strategy is suggested which concentrates on land consolidation and settlement with appropriate ownership patterns and other measures to increase the productivity of small farmers.

In our main research we review four possible alternative agricultural development strategies : *(a)* unimodal strategy ; *(b)* bimodal (dual) strategy ; *(c)* "industrialisation-first" strategy, i.e. discrimination against agriculture and the rural sector ; and *(d)* collectivisation or socialisation of rural areas.

Very briefly, the essence of the unimodal strategy is based on the progressive modernisation of agriculture "from the bottom up". In contrast with the bimodal strategy, which encourages the growth of the modern commercial, large-scale, relatively capital-intensive subsector of agriculture side by side with a traditional subsistence subsector, the unimodal approach relies on the widespread application of labour-intensive technology to the whole of agriculture. Through a combination of agricultural research, land redistribution, the provision of rural infrastructure, the growth of rural institutions and other measures, agricultural development is spread relatively evenly over the mass of the people. This strategy proved to be very successful in Japan (between about 1868 and the early 1950s). It can be argued that the unimodal strategy is likely to be the most appropriate for all three archetypes, given our preference for improvements in the living standards of the poor within a growth context. [1]

The bimodal structure and strategy is based on the promotion of a commercial, modern subsector which provides the bulk of agricultural output to satisfy the domestic and export demand for food and other agricultural products. The remainder of agriculture is confined to a traditional subsistence sector which has practically no claims on public resources.

The "industrialisation-first" strategy is based on the belief that industrialisation is the key to development and that the role of the industrial sector as the advanced sector is to pull behind it the backward agricultural sector. This strategy entails, inter alia, discriminating strongly against agriculture through a number of measures such as turning the

[1] It should be reiterated that the prevailing rural structure and rural strategy in any given country depends on a combination of historical factors, the political orientation of the régime, the policy maker's preference function and other initial conditions. All these have to be taken into account in formulating a strategy. What is suggested here is that a unimodal strategy may be the best envelope for somewhat different strategies fitting the case of three archetype regions.

internal terms of trade against it, promoting import-substituting industries through high protection, allocating only a minimal share of public resources to agriculture and not encouraging the development of rural institutions (India and Pakistan in the 1950s and 1960s were prototype examples of this strategy).

Finally, the socialisation and collectivisation of agriculture usually takes the form of collective or co-operative farms involving (a) the elimination of land ownership ; (b) the consolidation of land and other assets into "communes" or collectives which are run jointly and where the benefits are shared among members ; and (c) the undertaking of both farm and off-farm activities. [1]

It can be argued that, if the prevailing structure and development strategy is unimodal in nature, no conflict between the output and poverty reduction objectives need arise if the strategy is well conceived. However, if on the other hand the present structure is, and past strategy was, bimodal (or indeed of the "industrialisation-first" type), a conflict may arise over some transitional period during which major structural and institutional changes have to occur to convert a prevailing bimodal structure in agriculture to a more unimodal one. The policy package which suggests itself in this case consists of a combination of land reform (or changes in tenancy arrangements) complemented by a whole set of policy measures (and in some cases institutional changes) favourable to small farmers, landless workers and other rural groups which had previously been discriminated against. This set of complementary measures includes, inter alia, the provision of credit, extension services, an appropriate price policy which might be effective in encouraging the adoption of a more intermediate technology and a larger share of public investment projects directed towards traditional agriculture which would improve the infrastructure base available to the poor. [2]

In order to evaluate the over-all effects of such a policy package on an economy, it is fruitful to look at it within our interdependent consistency framework. If we start by describing the process from the production side, the major effect of this package is to generate a more equal income distribution partially because, as was seen in the previous section, rent income will be spread much more evenly than before the reform, partially because land is likely to be more intensively cultivated

---

[1] It should be noted that these strategies are not necessarily completely mutually exclusive, except between the unimodal and bimodal strategies.

[2] There might be instances in which both output and equity might be increased through a package of measures falling short of incorporating land reform. In general, however, the latter may be a precondition and a catalyst.

through the application of more labour per unit of land on smaller holdings. Furthermore, it is possible that as the size distribution of farms switches from a bimodal one to a unimodal one following land distribution, the average technology might become more labour intensive (with labour inputs replacing mechanical implements). As was discussed in the previous section, there are reasons to believe that aggregate output might remain at the same level as before the implementation of the new strategy—or that it might even fall slightly during a (relatively short) transitional period. [1]

An important secondary effect of the more equal personal income distribution in the rural areas is likely to be a rise in food demand since, as income rises, the demand for food becomes steadily less sensitive to changes in income. In turn, the combination of a rise in demand and constant (or slightly reduced) production should lead to higher agricultural prices relative to non-agricultural prices. This improvement in the internal terms of trade favouring agriculture is likely to benefit further the relative income position of the rural target groups.

In the same way, shifts in the composition of demand generated by a more equal income distribution tend to be reflected, in general, in a relative increase in the total consumption of labour-intensive as against capital-intensive commodities. Thus it appears that from the income and demand sides the secondary effects of a unimodal agricultural strategy tend to reinforce the primary production effects.

Two additional macroeconomic effects are worth noting in the process described above. First, the improvement in the relative income position of people in rural areas compared with that of urban workers is likely to lead to a reduction of rural-urban migration. Second, the inflationary impact of rising food prices could somewhat reduce the incomes of informal sector workers in urban areas, thereby dampening somewhat the positive distributional effects in agriculture. [2]

In this analysis of the effects of the new policy it has been assumed so far that no significant change in output would occur—at least during a transitional period. If, however, the comprehensive land reform package were so successful on the supply side that output were to rise in the post-reform period, this apparently blissful phenomenon might well turn

---

[1] Recent history provides many examples of inappropriate land reforms which led to a drastic fall in output. In these instances land reform failed because it was not accompanied by a set of complementary measures of the type previously discussed.

[2] Given the much larger number of individuals in the rural target groups in most developing countries than in the urban informal sector, the over-all personal (or household) income distribution should become significantly more even in the post-reform period.

78

out to have perverse effects on distribution. Indeed, a rise in agricultural output in the context of an income and price inelastic demand and limited scope for either import substitution or exports would be likely to lead to lower agricultural prices and a lower value of total agricultural production than before the reform. The ultimate impact on rural income distribution would depend on the magnitude of the above factors in addition to the share of income accruing to the target groups out of value added and the ratio of the latter to gross output before and after the reform.

The few attempts at modelling rural development within a general consistency, multisectoral framework seem to agree that the price and income inelastic nature of agricultural demand is a (if not the) major constraint on agricultural development and the achievement of a more equal income distribution. Consequently, in those countries where there is some scope for import substitution of food, such a strategy might allow the demand constraint to be relaxed—at least until self-sufficiency is reached. This strategy might entail a trade-off between efficiency goals, on the one hand, and employment and distributional objectives, on the other. Of course, an even more preferable alternative—if feasible—would be the export promotion of agricultural commodities.

A final consequence of the land reform package that is worth noting involves savings. It is likely that savings in the rural sector will be increasingly channelled into investment within this sector rather than transferred to other sectors. The small farmers' security of ownership might provide them with a strong incentive for various accretionary activities. More specifically, as was pointed out previously, many savings decisions are equivalent to investment decisions in small-scale agriculture. Activities such as farm improvement, land levelling, the construction of mini-irrigation canals and storage capacity on small farms are tantamount to savings-cum-investment decisions.[1] The net result of these changes—although difficult to predict accurately on an *a priori* basis— should be an increase in capital formation in agriculture and a positive effect on land and labour productivity. Consequently, if the total flow of savings remains the same after the reform as before, the agricultural sector will provide a smaller flow of savings to the rest of the economy.

The implications of this potential reduction in the transfer of the "agricultural surplus" to other sectors need not be alarming for at least

[1] Another form of forced savings which, however, represents a flow from agriculture to other sectors is represented by the land payments which the new farmers have to make to the previous large landlords (assuming that a compensatory scheme is in existence).

two reasons. First, to the extent that more capital formation in agriculture results in rising agricultural output and productivity, the traditional role of agriculture as a provider of capital to industry can be performed at a later stage through such mechanisms as lower relative food prices. Second, the experience of the past 25 years bears out the dismal consequences for agricultural output of discriminating against agriculture too early in the development process and strangling, as it were, the goose before it has had a chance to lay the golden egg.

In conclusion, land redistribution, if it is accompanied by a series of complementary measures to form a consistent land reform package, may well be a necessary precondition to the joint achievement of growth and distributional equity, at least in those countries or regions where a bimodal agricultural structure and agricultural development strategy prevail.

One interesting effect of a rural development-oriented strategy is on the size and pattern of migration. Figure 8 illustrates the changes in the pattern under a growth-oriented bimodal strategy and under a unimodal strategy. The bimodal structure before the rural-based strategy is implemented shows a clear compartmentalisation between modern and traditional agriculture. After the unimodal strategy has taken hold the distinction between these two subsectors may disappear gradually (hence the deletion of the line between these two subsectors in the lower part of figure 8) and the number of landless farmers will be reduced, through increased employment. In addition to a substantial reduction in the flow of rural-urban migration, a circular, balanced, essentially seasonal migration pattern can occur between rural agricultural and non-agricultural activities. This flow depends on the seasonal employment pattern in agriculture discussed below. A net outflow from agricultural activities to rural off-farm activities is likely to occur as well as a continuing but reduced flow to the informal urban and modern sectors. The probability of these migrants obtaining productive jobs is increased, given the reduction in their number over time.

A number of problems connected with the implementation of the unimodal strategy can only be touched upon here. A first difficulty is that of mounting a frontal attack in terms of a policy package consisting of measures such as land and structural reforms, institutional changes, price policies and research in a synchronised way. Second, one key to the success of rural development depends on the achievement of a mutually reinforcing relationship between agricultural and rural non-agricultural activities. It is essential that the off-farm activities be designed in such a way as to be seasonally complementary from an effective

Figure 8. Migration pattern under bimodal structure before and after structural changes

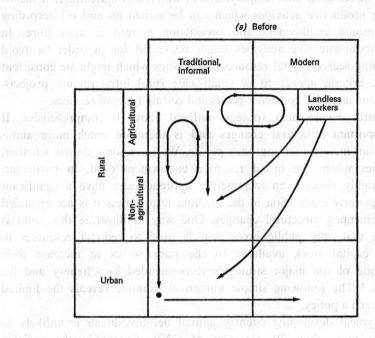

(a) Before

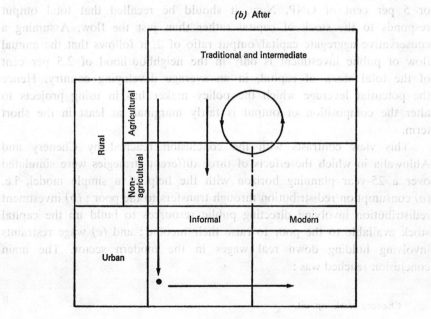

(b) After

employment standpoint with the agricultural activities. Given the very high level of seasonal underemployment in traditional agriculture, it means identifying productive activities which can be turned on and off according to the seasonal employment and production pattern in agriculture. In general, labour-intensive activities might be called for in order to avoid underutilising scarce capital resources. Activities which might be consistent with those criteria appear to be small-scale rural infrastructure projects, roads, labour-intensive consumer goods and certain types of services.

The rural development strategy outlined above is comprehensive. It entails important structural changes and is therefore much more ambitious than an incremental approach *per se*. We have some doubts whether, in countries where the initial resource endowment (and, in particular, land) is highly skewed, an incremental approach can have a significant effect on poverty eradication in the medium term unless it is accompanied by complementary structural changes. One way to illustrate this point is to assume that only public investment is used to redirect resources to raise the capital stock available to the poor so as to increase their income—one of the major strategies recommended by Chenery and his co-authors. [1] The following simple numerical example reveals the limited effects of such a policy.

In a typical developing country annual net investment is unlikely to amount to more than 20 per cent of GNP. Except in the socialist countries public investment may represent one-fourth of total investment or 5 per cent of GNP. Now, it should be recalled that total output responds to the stock of capital rather than just the flow. Assuming a conservative aggregate capital/output ratio of 2, it follows that the annual flow of public investment is only in the neighbourhood of 2.5 per cent of the total stock of capital, in an average developing country. Hence the potential leverage which the policy maker has in using projects to alter the composition of output is fairly marginal, at least in the short term.

This view contrasts with the conclusion reached by Chenery and Ahluwalia in which the effects of three different strategies were simulated over a 25-year planning horizon with the help of a simple model, i.e. *(a)* consumption redistribution through transfers to the poor ; *(b)* investment redistribution involving directing public resources to build up the capital stock available to the poor to raise their income ; and *(c)* wage restraints involving holding down real wages in the modern sector. The main conclusion reached was :

---

[1] Chenery *et al.*, op. cit.

there is considerable potential for raising income in low-income groups through a policy of "investment transfers". Such a strategy, although operating at the margin, can achieve substantial improvements in patterns of asset concentration over time. If income in the poorer groups is constrained by lack of physical and human capital and access to infrastructure, then reallocation of public resources can provide a powerful mechanism for removing these constraints. The extent of resource transfer involved—2 per cent of GNP per year for 25 years—is not small, but is should be feasible in many countries. [1]

There are perhaps two reasons for the more positive assessment of the effects of a policy of public investment reallocation in the above study than the one we have offered here. First, the size of investment transfers amounting to 2 per cent of GNP—corresponding to 1 per cent of the stock of capital in our previous example, or 40 per cent of the total assumed level of public investment—would require a very major commitment to poverty reduction on the part of the policy maker sustained over a considerable period of time. [2] Second, the three strategies referred to above are all incremental in nature, so that the conclusion, in fact, is that among possible incremental measures, investment transfers may be the most appropriate to achieve some degree of income redistribution.

Although the rural strategy can be considered the major pillar of the over-all development strategy, there are other pillars, two of which might be touched upon briefly here.

The first relates to the need for an appropriate strategy with respect to the informal urban sector. A number of the ILO comprehensive employment strategy mission reports have emphasised the important potential role which the informal sector can play in development. Basically, it embraces traditional urban activities and small-scale rural non-agricultural activities. In general, these activities are characterised by *(a)* ease of entry ; *(b)* reliance on indigenous resources ; *(c)* family ownership of enterprises ; *(d)* small scale of operation ; *(e)* labour-intensive and adapted technology ; *(f)* skills acquired outside the formal school system ; and *(g)* unregulated and competitive markets. [3]

It is argued that the informal sector can make key contributions to output and employment—partially, at least, through the inter-relationships

---

[1] See M. S. Ahluwalia and H. Chenery : "A model of distribution and growth", in Chenery *et al., op. cit.*, pp. 234-235.

[2] Incidentally, if such a commitment were present might it not be realistic to assume that structural changes and reforms (e.g. land distribution) might be implemented jointly with incremental measures by the government in question ?

[3] See ILO : *Employment, incomes and equality : a strategy for increasing productive employment in Kenya* (Geneva, 1972), p. 6.

and linkages which are said to exist between formal and informal sectors. In this connection our SAM framework lends itself particularly well to a quantitative examination of these linkages since production activities are broken down according to product, technology and form of organisation. Hence the effects of increased output of informal activities can be traced through the system.

An interesting point with regard to the informal sector (which applies also to the traditional agricultural sector) is that the factor prices which it faces tend to correspond much more closely to the scarcity value of the factors (or their efficiency or shadow price) than do the set of factor prices applying to the modern sector. Thus small firms and self-employed activities in the informal sector are much more likely to use resources efficiently (by pricing them at their shadow prices) than larger firms, which allocate on the basis of (distorted) market prices and the maximisation of private profits.

A final element of an appropriate development strategy which might be mentioned is the desirability of replacing the import-substitution phase by an export-substitution phase. The high efficiency cost of the former has been well documented in the literature. When high protective walls were built to discourage imports, not only were scarce resources often wasted (as reflected in some instances by negative value added when inputs and outputs are valued at world prices) but also the distortion of prices generated by import-substitution measures encouraged the adoption of relatively capital-intensive technologies. These technologies, in turn, contributed to the employment problem and a skewed income distribution.

In contrast, an export-substitution phase would concentrate on trying to replace traditional exports by labour-intensive manufactured exports. It is, of course, clear that the successful implementation of such an export strategy would be greatly helped by the institution of preferential measures by developed countries which would facilitate the entry of these exports in their own markets. This brings us to one of the elements of the "new international economic order", which it is not our brief to discuss here. Suffice it to say that, since the "rest of the world" is an intrinsic part of our framework, with its own set of accounts, the effects on the whole system of new policies originating abroad could be analysed, at least in their general outline.

APPENDIX: A TECHNICAL DESCRIPTION OF THE SOCIAL ACCOUNTING MATRIX

AN APPLICATION OF A BASIC SOCIAL ACCOUNTING MATRIX TO SRI LANKA

Table 6 applies the basic format of the SAM, reproduced in tables 2 and 3, to the specific case of Sri Lanka. [1]

Reading across row 1 of the table, urban labour earns wages equal to 1,673 (in millions of rupees). These come from all production activities, but the most important are trade and private transport services (414) and government services (555). These are also important sources of earned income for rural labour (row 2). For them, however, rice cultivation (706) is also highly significant. The estate labour force (row 3) earns income primarily on the tea plantations (526). Thus the table captures the relationship between the structure of production and the sources of wages and jobs in different labour markets. It also shows how private profits (4,984 in total) tend to be concentrated in "other agriculture" (vegetables, spices, fruits) and in trade and private transport services. The surpluses of state-owned enterprises add up to 174 net, there being some industries, such as trade and construction transport, in which state enterprise makes a loss. In general the top right-hand corner of table 6 shows how much factor income is generated in the economy, the production activities it is generated by, and the factorial income distribution, i.e. the extent to which each factor of production receives a share of this income. This is the main part of national income accounting by sector of origin and of the distribution of income according to factor shares. Through the recognition of different parts of the labour market the dependence of each on different production activities can be recorded. The simplest example is that the estate labour force depends essentially on the tea industry (and to a lesser extent on rubber) for its employment.

The incomes of the six factors of production are laid out in the first six columns. Thus all urban labour income (1,673) goes to urban households. For rental income and private profits the allocation is more difficult: it depends on who owns the corresponding factors, since rents go to the owners of housing while profits go to the owners of capital, i.e. to companies or to the household owners of unincorporated businesses.

The current accounts for institutions show three sorts of household, two types of companies and government. This sixfold classification is the analogue here of Gregory King's classification in table 1. (It could obviously

---

[1] See Pyatt and Roe, op. cit., for a full discussion. The basic table from which table 6 is derived has about four times as many accounts and is therefore much more detailed.

Table 6. A social accounting matrix for Sri Lanka, 1970
(in millions of rupees)

		Expenditures									
		1 — Factors of production						2 — Institutions			3
		Labour			Other			Current accounts			
								Households			Private corporations
Receipts		Urban	Rural	Estate	Housing	Other private	Public	Urban	Rural	Estate	Private corporations
1 Factors of production — Labour — Urban											
Rural											
Estate											
Other — Housing											
Other private											
Public											
2 Institutions — Current accounts — Households — Urban		1673				137	662				434
Rural			3185			330	3026				203
Estate				711		31	30				7
3 Private corporations						135	1266				
State corporations							174				
Government								368	194	4	272
4 / 5 Combined capital account								519	807	11	527
6 Production activities — Tea								14	55	7	
Rubber											
Coconuts								54	208	27	
Rice								158	760	102	
Other agriculture								357	980	139	
Food and drink								253	541	82	
Other industry								258	621	69	
Construction											
Trade and transport								410	1074	122	
Private services								405	920	85	
Government services											
7 Rest of the world								207	741	143	
Totals		1673	3185	711	633	498	4174	3003	6901	791	1443

Expenditures — Columns: **4** Institutions (Current accounts): State corporations, Government · **5** Combined capital assets · **6** Production activities · **7** Rest of the world

State corporations	Government	Combined capital assets	Tea	Rubber	Coconuts	Rice	Other agriculture	Food and drink	Other industry	Trade and construction transport	Trade and private transport services	Private services	Government services	Rest of the world	Totals
			5	5	9	25	75	46	182	81	414	276	555		1673
			43	158	67	706	247	68	259	159	487	276	715		3185
			526	133	11		5	4	2	5	8	12	5		711
												633			633
			13	24	442	282	1259	184	604	742	1424	123		−113	4984
							11	12	109	−8	−1	73			174
	91													6	3003
	151													6	6901
	6													6	791
	57													−15	1443
	237														411
104		313	33	4	14	10	19	288	216	66	130	76	29	94	2234
307	43													425	2639
		−55										2	2	839	864
		25												341	374
		29							8			6	4	2	577
		105				1082		239	8			15	18		2242
			11	1		2	95	63	34	3		39	16	106	1846
		37				9	11	24	188			29	8	94	1276
		72	97	24	9	35	69	49	554	417	172	37	66	241	2790
		1595							1			50	92		1745
		154	50	10	8	44	23	95	249	206	96	42	59	203	2845
			11	3	7	15	1		4	9	38	55	37	287	1877
	1649														1649
		364	75	12	10	32	53	204	370	65	70	133	43		2522
411	2234	2639	864	374	577	2242	1846	1276	2790	1745	2845	1877	1649	2522	

be more detailed by allowing a higher degree of disaggregation (i.e. more household types) but this would detract from the principles of table 6, on which we want to concentrate.) The row sums for the institutions show their total incomes. These come primarily from supplying factor services but there are also incomes received from other institutions (i.e. transfer payments). These are primarily profit distributed by companies, benefits paid by government, and tax payments to government.

The brief discussion of the top half of table 6 suggests that the distribution of income can be looked at in a more consolidated form in terms of table 7 (this last table represents a numerical application of table 3). It was shown in Chapter 2 that tables 3 and 7 indicate explicitly the transformation of the structure of production into the factorial income distribution (in the northeast quadrant). In the northwest quadrant this total income is allocated to the institutions (including household groups which provide the factor services). Hence the distribution of wealth (including human skills and capital) together with the structure of production underlies this northwest quadrant. Finally, in the southwest quadrant, transfer payments are incorporated, i.e. taxation, government social security payments and profit distribution of disposable incomes between institutions (and household groups). For example, table 7 shows that in Sri Lanka rural households had a disposable income of 6,763 million rupees in 1970.

DESCRIPTION OF A COMPREHENSIVE SOCIAL ACCOUNTING MATRIX SCHEMA

In table 4 we presented a complete SAM which incorporates all the modules of our conceptual framework. In particular, the format of the SAM in table 4 includes the distribution of assets, factors and financial claims and a special account for "wants". This last account was described in some detail in Chapter 2 since it is central to an approach focused on the satisfaction of basic needs. Consequently the following description of table 4 carries on from where we left it in Chapter 2, i.e. after having explained the "wants" account.

The money received (from households) to pay for their wants in row 1 is exactly matched by expenditures on commodities in column 1. Thus, to satisfy wants for food, expenditures on different food items must be incurred. Similarly, the commodity "educational services" must be bought to satisfy wants for "education". This translation from wants to commodities is important to our subsequent analysis. Implicit in it is the effect of changes in incomes and prices on commodity expenditures by households.

Row 2 is a classification of the factors of production as in table 2, and as in table 4 shows factors as receiving income as payment for factor services, primarily from domestic production activities. In column 2 these incomes are paid out to the institutions which provide the factor services—labour incomes to households and profits to companies. Similarly, rows 3 to 5 and columns 3 to 5 of table 4 correspond to the treatment in table 2, with their intersection including all the current transfers in the economy. Several points are worth noting. First, in row 3, column 5 households receive the value of government services provided to them free, as well as transfers such as social security benefits. These incomes therefore contribute to the totals available to finance expenditures on wants in row 1, column 3. Other expenditures are in the form of direct taxes paid to government, while the remaining income is saved, i.e. it takes the form of a transfer from the

Table 7. An income distribution analysis table for Sri Lanka, 1970 (in millions of rupees)

			Rest of the world	Production activities											Totals	Institutions current accounts					
				Government services	Private services	Trade and transport	Construction	Other industry	Food and drink	Other agriculture	Rice	Coconuts	Rubber	Tea		Government	State corporations	Private corporations	Estate	Rural	Urban
Factors of production	Labour	Urban		555	276	414	81	182	46	75	25	9	5	5	1673						
		Rural		715	276	487	159	259	68	247	706	67	158	43	3185						
		Estate		5	12	8	5	2	4	5		11	133	526	711						
	Other	Housing			633										633						
		Other private			123	1424	742	604	184	1259	282	442	24	13	4984						
		Public			73	−1	−8	109	12	−11					174						
		Totals	−113	1275	1393	2332	979	1156	314	1575	1013	529	320	587	11360						
Institutions current accounts	Households	Urban	−6												2708	91		137	137	330	137
		Rural	−6												6763	151		135	31	3026	662
		Estate	−6												780	6		31	30		
	Private corporations		15												525		174				
	State corporations														307	57	70	1266		140	295
	Government		−94												374	237	104	272	11		
Rest of the world			−97													−448		468			
		Totals	−113															174	2183	6407	767
																		2472	6541	772

household current accounts, column 3, to the household capital accounts, row 6.

In row 4 the company sector should ideally be disaggregated to distinguish foreign companies, which typically endeavour to remit their profits abroad, and state-owned enterprises, which can be regarded as transferring all their profits to government. These types of company, together with private domestic companies (both incorporated and unincorporated), receive the operating surpluses of domestic production activities. They may also receive current transfers from government and some (net) income from abroad. This is paid out as distributed profits to domestic owners or as direct taxes to government. Otherwise, company incomes are retained as a transfer from their current account to their capital account.

Government revenue is restricted in row 5 to direct tax revenue : receipts from indirect taxes are treated as a negative expenditure in column 5. Genuine current expenditures are transfers to households and to companies, and expenditures on items such as defence and police services which are not captured in row 3 as direct benefits to particular household groups. The balancing item is the current account surplus, which is transferred to the government capital account in row 8.

The information in the first five rows and columns of table 4 give details on many key issues. These have already been noted with reference to living standards and poverty. We can now note that the additional information in rows 3 and 5 and columns 3 and 5 covers the distribution of income, as in table 3 ; domestic consumption and savings ; and both government current revenue by source and government expenditure by purpose.

In table 2 there is just one capital account. This is expanded to six accounts in table 4 (numbered 6 to 11), reflecting the importance of capital and wealth to a discussion of inequality. The first three of these (rows 6 to 8) are the capital accounts of the domestic institutions, and they receive domestic savings from their respective current accounts. Their other receipts are from columns 9 and 10, which are crucial. Account 9 refers to domestic factor endowments. The classification within this account covers the real wealth of the economy in terms of the educational and skill attainments of the population ; natural resources, such as land and mineral deposits, stocks of raw materials and finished products ; and fixed capital of various types such as houses, offices, roads, factories, vehicles, industrial plant and agricultural implements. At the beginning of the accounting period (usually one year, but a five-year plan period is possible), there is an initial stock of these assets which is owned by households, companies or government. This initial ownership of real assets is recorded in column 9, rows 6 to 8.

In addition to real assets, wealth may be held in the form of financial claims. These are money (i.e. paper) claims on other domestic institutions or on foreign institutions. They include money as such, bank accounts, insurance policies, government securities, corporation stock, and so on. If they are added to wealth held as real assets, the total wealth distribution is obtained. From this the distribution of net worth can be derived by subtracting from the wealth of each institution the financial claims on it which are held by other institutions. In row 11, column 10, appear financial claims on domestic institutions which are held by foreigners.

If savings during a year are added to wealth at the beginning of the year, the result is wealth at the end of the year. This is the arithmetical meaning of accounts 6 to 8. The revised distribution of wealth held as factors of production is recorded in row 9, while reversed wealth held as financial claims is in row 10.

The difference between initial factor endowments and revised endowments is investment. The purchases of commodities appear in row 14. They are financed either by savings or by borrowing, and hence by incurring a new financial liability. The latter is recorded at the intersection of row 10 and column 10, and is therefore an element in the flow of funds. It can be noted that government is in a particularly privileged position here : it can invent a new financial claim on itself. If others will buy it through increased savings (decreased consumption) or through decreased investment, then government can use the money to finance its own investment or current spending without inflationary consequences.

The capital account for the rest of the world, row 11 and column 11, is balanced by flows of financial and real resources, e.g. capital transfers and the current account surplus or deficit. This arises mainly from the balance of trade, so that if imports exceed exports the trade balance is negative. This deficit will be further increased if net income from abroad is negative. The two combined give the over-all deficit, which requires a capital transfer from the rest of the world to finance it. Thus a deficit implies that financial claims by foreigners on domestic institutions have increased.

The discussion of the accounts in table 4 is completed by reference to those for production activities and commodities. The former receive revenue in row 13 by selling different commodities. Their costs, in column 13, are payments to factors (which include operating surpluses) and purchases of commodities for use as raw materials.

Row 14 records all the different commodities that the economy requires : consumption goods to satisfy wants ; non-personal government services ; investment goods ; exports ; and raw materials. These are supplied in column 14, either by producing them domestically or by importing. These are the only sources of goods in physical units. But table 4 is balanced in financial terms. Expenditures on commodities are at market prices, while production activities are paid producer prices for what they deliver, and imports are valued at the cost of goods when they arrive. Indirect taxes, subsidies, import duties, etc., must therefore be added. These items, in row 15, column 14, complete the table.